SCROLLSAWS

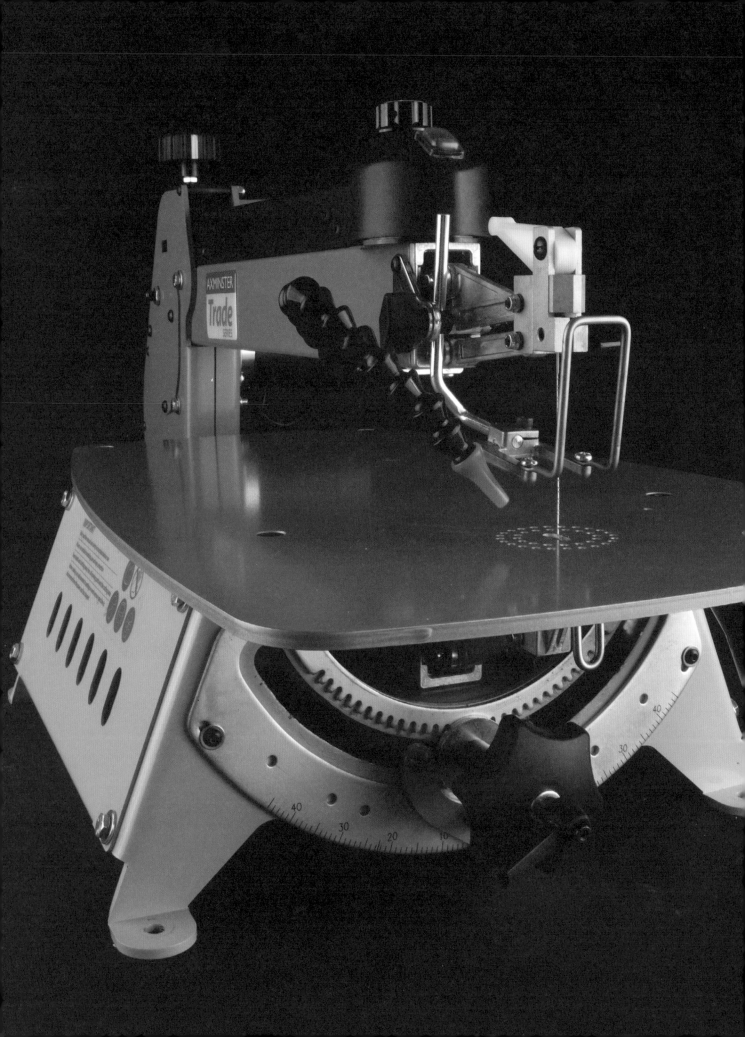

SCROLLSAWS

A WOODWORKER'S GUIDE

FRED AND JULIE BYRNE

GUILD OF MASTER CRAFTSMAN PUBLICATIONS LTD

First published 2018 by
Guild of Master Craftsman Publications Ltd
Castle Place, 166 High Street,
Lewes, East Sussex BN7 1XU

Previously published as *Success with Scrollsaws* (first published 2006)

ISBN 978 1 78494 443 8

Publisher: Jonathan Bailey
Production: Jim Bulley, Jo Pallet
Senior Project Editor: Virginia Brehaut
Managing Art Editor: Gilda Pacitti
Designer: Ginny Zeal
Photography: Julie & Fred Byrne
Additional photography: GMC Publications/
Anthony Bailey (cover and all full-page photographs;
also pages 14, 18 and 26), Derek Jones (page 27),
Hegner UK (page 12–13)
Illustrations: Fred and Julie Byrne

Colour origination by GMC Reprographics
Printed and bound in China

CONTENTS

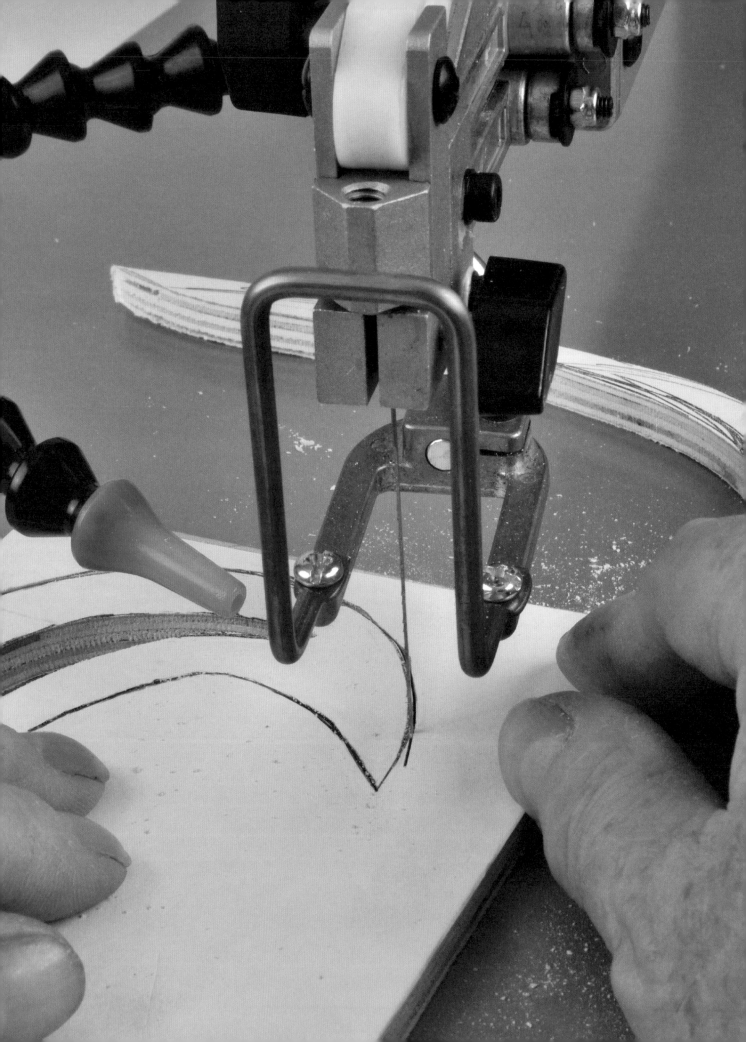

Introduction

The scrollsaw has evolved over the centuries from the simple hand-held fretsaw to the fine electrical saws we enjoy today. In its modern form it has grown in popularity because it is simple to master and enables even inexperienced workers to create a wide range of useful and decorative items around the home. The scrollsaw can shape many different materials, both thin and thick, into chunky designs or intricate works of art.

Part 1 describes the basic equipment and techniques that you need to get started. We have not recommended particular makes or models, because new ones are being introduced all the time and this information would quickly go out of date. Instead, we describe the features to look out for when purchasing a saw, so that you can make an informed choice for yourself. The technique of scrollsawing is not difficult; the guidance we have given should start you on the right track, but practice is the main thing.

The rest of the book is given over to a selection of themed projects for different parts of the house, which will give you ample practice in the techniques described. You can follow the projects exactly, or customize them by mixing and matching motifs if you feel more adventurous. We hope you will get as much pleasure as we do from this absorbing craft.

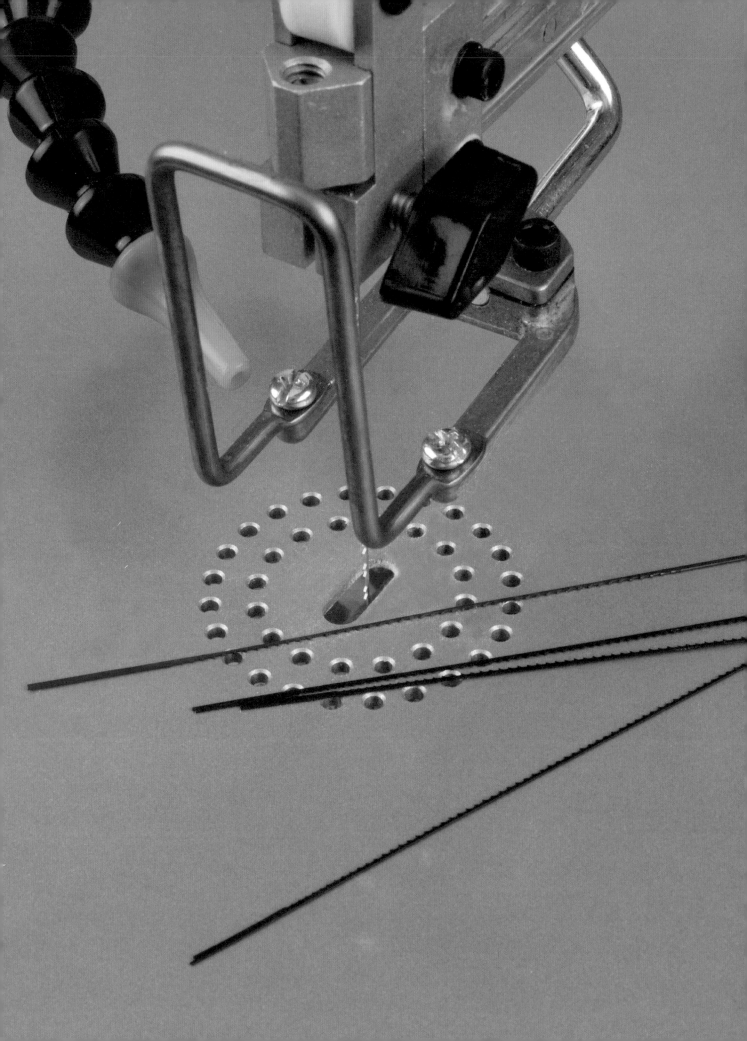

1
Tools, Techniques & Materials

1:1
Introducing the scrollsaw

1:2
Other equipment and materials

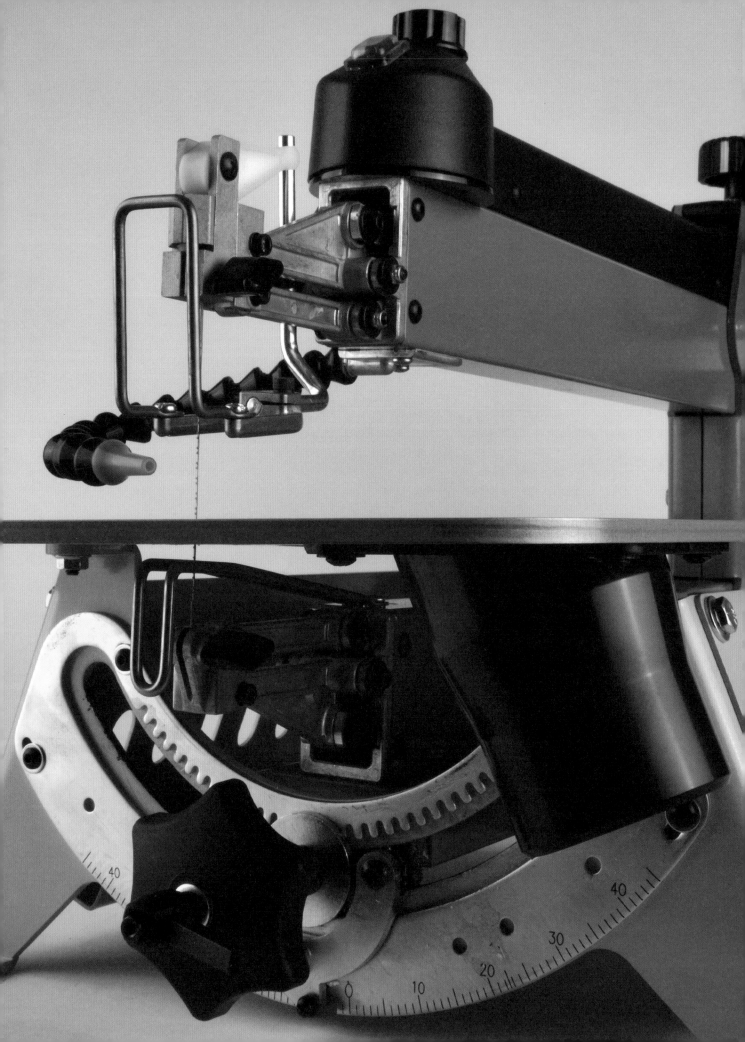

1:1
Introducing the scrollsaw

The scrollsaw is essentially a motorized fretsaw – and it is still sometimes called a fretsaw, especially in the UK. It is a comparatively small machine that can be mounted on a purpose-made stand or on an ordinary workbench, and is the perfect tool for the freehand cutting of inlay and fretwork in relatively thin wood (up to about 2in or 50mm thick) and certain other materials. Its narrow blade enables it to cut tight curves or sharp angles when required, and internal cut-outs can also be made. It is not suited for speed-cutting thick woods, for which a larger tool such as a bandsaw or a tablesaw would be much more appropriate.

We will start by looking at the features of the scrollsaw itself, then, just as important, the different kinds of blades that can be used with it. We then review some of the most useful accessories that are available from scrollsaw manufacturers; depending on which make you buy, some accessories may come with the saw and others may have to be bought separately as and when you need them. Scrollsaw technique comes easily with practice, but we offer some guidance to get you started. We finish this section with advice on safety; the scrollsaw is one of the safest of power tools when it is used correctly, but like all machinery it does need to be treated with respect.

Naming of parts

The table supports the workpiece while you cut. It can be made from aluminium or cast iron, and can be tilted in one direction or in both directions, depending on which make and model you choose, in order to make bevel or compound cuts. You control the direction of cutting by turning the workpiece on the table as the work proceeds. To help the workpiece move around smoothly, apply a thin coat of wax polish to the table top; allow this to dry, then buff up.

The interchangeable blades for the machine are very thin, making the scrollsaw an ideal tool for cutting patterns in a variety of materials. Blade choice is discussed on pages 16–17.

All scrollsaws have a power switch of some kind – either a single on–off switch or separate on and off buttons. Some also have a variable-speed control. A foot-controlled on–off pedal can be fitted as an accessory.

The hold-down arm, which resembles the 'foot' of a sewing machine, is an optional accessory that helps with the cutting of thin materials, and also acts to some extent as a blade guard.

The dust blower fitted to most models is operated by bellows and keeps the saw line clear of dust so you can see what you are doing. Some models have a dust extraction port, and when a vacuum unit is attached to this the blowing action is converted to suction.

The model you choose may not have all the features of the Hegner scrollsaw illustrated here, and the layout of the controls may be different, but the basic principles will be the same.

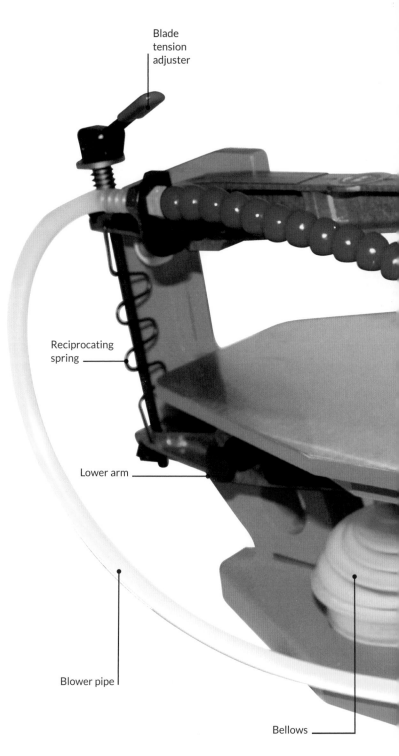

Blade tension adjuster

Reciprocating spring

Lower arm

Blower pipe

Bellows

ABOVE *The principal parts of a typical modern scrollsaw, the Hegner Multicut 1, a 14in (355mm) model.*

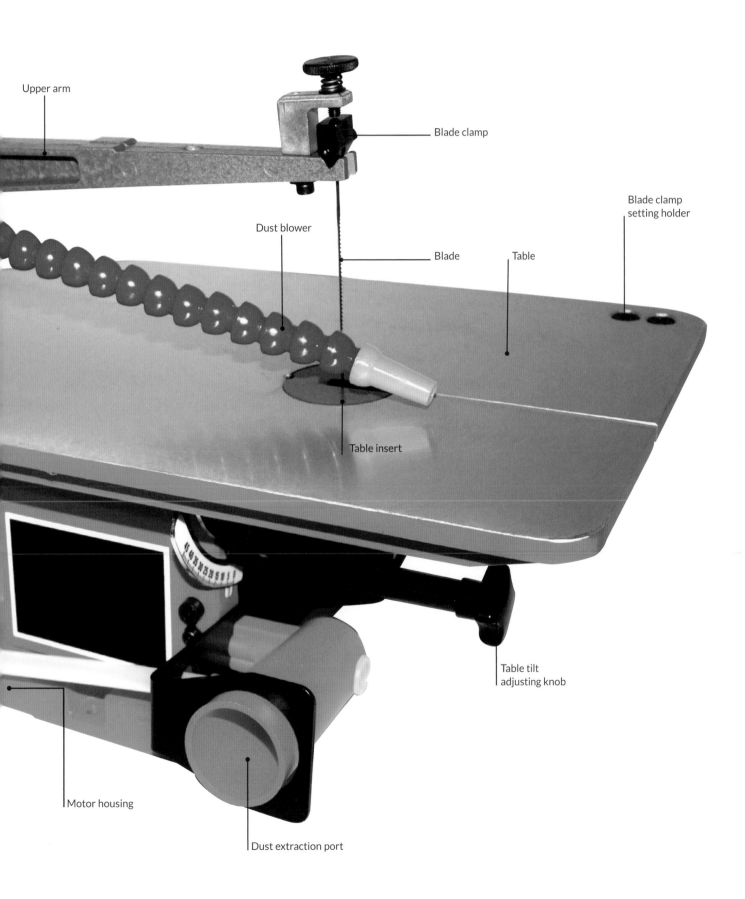

Upper arm

Blade clamp

Blade clamp
setting holder

Dust blower

Blade

Table

Table insert

Table tilt
adjusting knob

Motor housing

Dust extraction port

Choosing a scrollsaw

There are a number of factors to consider when choosing which scrollsaw to buy; here are the points that we have found to be particularly important.

Scrollsaws vary quite a lot in price and quality, and we would always recommend purchasing the best one you can afford. The price itself is generally a good measure of the quality of the tool. A well-made saw will feel solid and will not have excessive play in the arms and other moving parts. Overall weight varies from about 38lb (17kg) to 62lb (28kg), which may be an important consideration if you need to move the saw often. Most models are equipped with a 100-watt or $^1/_{10}$-horsepower induction motor, but the heavier industrial machines may be 160W or $^1/_4$hp. We advise that you never purchase a scrollsaw without seeing it in action first. A well-balanced tool will run smoothly, with very little vibration.

Both stand- and bench-mounted models are equally suitable, so long as they are well bolted down to minimize vibration and set at a comfortable working height for you, whether you prefer to stand or sit at your work.

Points to consider

· **Throat capacity** is the measurement from the blade to the arm support at the back of the machine. This measurement is particularly important because it determines the length of material that can be cut without reversing the work. Smaller models have a capacity of 14in (355mm), whereas some of the larger ones can measure 22in (560mm). The maximum thickness of material that can be cut is usually around 2in (50mm), whichever model you choose.

LEFT *The Axminster Trade Series EX-21 Scroll Saw, 21in (535mm) throat capacity.*

· **Blade suspension** is important, as you will need to use different sizes of blade and to replace them when they snap. Quick-release blade clamps will save a lot of time when making inside cuts, where the blade has to be threaded through a pre-drilled hole. A forward-mounted tension adjuster will also make the blade-changing process much easier. There are two main types of blade available to you – plain-end and pin-end – and this may influence your choice of saw, although some models can accept both types. Plain-end blades are held in place with clamps, and are widely available in many different varieties; they are a favourite with long-standing woodworkers. Pin-end blades have cross-pins through each end (as on a coping saw) that rest in a holder or hook onto the saw; they are much easier to change, but there is less choice available, and they tend to be coarser than the plain-end blades.

· Scrollsaws come with one or two **speed settings**, or with continuously variable speeds. A high speed of 1200–1800 strokes per minute is ideal for cutting hard woods. A low speed of 400–800 strokes per minute is best for cutting softwood like pine, which is our wood of choice when using the scrollsaw. In our opinion a scrollsaw with variable speeds is preferable, as you then have the best of both worlds.

We strongly recommend that you thoroughly research all the options available to you before purchasing. Websites such as those listed on page 172 can help you with this, and you should also look out for the comparative reviews which appear from time to time in the woodworking press. The big woodworking shows are a great opportunity to examine the current models in the flesh, and maybe even try them out before you make your decision.

Useful questions

How much money do I want to spend?
The general rule is to buy the best you can afford, but there is a healthy secondhand market via the Internet, worth investigating. If you are new to scrollsawing and do not yet know if you will like it then a cheaper one would suffice, but if scrolling is your passion, get the best you can.

What kind of scrolling do I plan to do?
If you plan to do a lot of fretwork, you will probably be repositioning the blade often, so a quick blade change will be important. You will also need a scrollsaw that takes plain-end blades, not pin-end blades, as the cross endpin will not pass through a small blade starter hole that some fine fretwork patterns require.

Are bevelled/angled cuts important?
On the majority of scrollsaws the table will tilt to both the left and right. Sometimes you are working at such an angle that it's hard work keeping the saw on the cutting line, so a saw with a tilting arm may be beneficial.

What thickness of wood will I normally be working with?
If the wood is thin you'll need a zero clearance insert within the table, to both support your fragile work and stop any small pieces falling through the slot for the blade. If using thick wood (the maximum being about 2in/50mm) make sure the saw has ample power to cope.

What size of project will you make?
This is where you'll want to take the throat capacity into consideration, the measurement from the back of the arm support to the blade.

Blade selection

We have already looked at the two different systems of blade attachment, pin-end and plain-end (see page 15). Now we will look at the types of blade that could be used to complete the projects in this book.

Teeth per inch

The coarseness or fineness of any saw blade is traditionally defined by the number of teeth per inch (tpi; 1in = 25mm). Scrollsaw blades, however, are designated by a single number, and the general rule is that the higher the number, the coarser the blade – in other words, the fewer teeth it has per inch. The number of tpi varies from one manufacturer to another, but the table below gives an indication of the typical range. To complete all of the projects in the book you will need a small selection of nos. 7, 5 and 1. In general terms, the no. 7 blades are used for cutting thick and hard woods, while nos. 5 to 1 are for cutting softer woods and making fine and intricate cuts. The finer blades will leave a smoother finish, but may dull and break more quickly.

ABOVE *A selection of blades:* **1** *precision ground tooth, skip reverse,* **2** *crown tooth,* **3** *double tooth,* **4** *mach speed and* **5** *spiral.*

Blade no.	Teeth per inch (25mm)
12	9.5–12
7	11.5–14
5	12–16
1	20–25

Key point

Practise using different blade sizes to see which ones suit you. Using a large blade to cut thin material will just rip it up, whereas a thin blade will snap if used in thick material. You need to find the one that gives the desired finish without making the saw work too hard.

Blade types

- **Standard blades** have teeth that all face downwards; they give a smooth, fine cut, and are the most commonly used type.

- **Reverse-tooth blades** have some teeth at the bottom that face upwards. This again gives a smooth cut, with minimal splintering on the underside of the work, so little sanding is needed.

- **Skip-tooth blades** have spaces between the teeth to clear the sawdust more easily; they cut fast and keep burning to a minimum, but the standard ones may leave a rough edge that will require sanding.

- **Spiral blades** have their teeth wound around a central cylinder, and enable you to cut in any direction. The idea is good, but these blades tend to dull and snap quickly and can be difficult to control.

- **Crown-tooth blades** are a unique tooth design that cut on both the up and down strokes, allowing for a very smooth controlled cut. An economic blade that can be turned upside down for a fresh set of teeth.

- **Double-tooth blades** are a set of two teeth together and then a space, expelling the sawdust and helping to keep heat out of the blade.

- **Mach-speed blades** have wide-spaced, ultra-sharp teeth for fast accurate cuts with minimized burning.

If you have a need to cut metal or plastic, there are blades on the market that are especially designed for these materials.

Installing the blade

First check that the table is in the horizontal (0°) position, then, using the key supplied by the manufacturer, secure the blade clamps to each end of the blade, making sure the teeth are facing downwards. Then fit the blade, with the clamps attached, onto the scrollsaw mountings. Use a small try square or triangle to align the blade at a right angle to the table. Tighten the blade and then flick the back of it with your finger; if it is right you should hear a clear 'ping'. If the blade is not tight enough it will easily wander off the line. When you are satisfied, tighten down the spring on the top blade clamp. Slacken off the blade when it is not in use.

For all of the inlay projects it is very important that the edges of each piece are cut square; otherwise they will not butt together flush. To double-check the squareness of the blade, saw a small piece of wood in half, turn one of the pieces over, and if it still lines up with the other piece you know the blade is square. If not, undo the blade and repeat the setting-up procedure until you get it right.

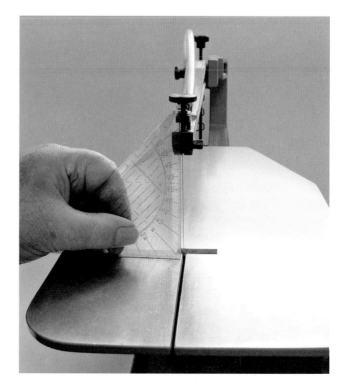

ABOVE *Using a set square to check blade alignment.*

Some useful accessories

There are many accessories on the market that may promote your safety and enhance your use of the saw. You will not need them all, but here are a few that are worth considering.

· **Quick-release blade clamps** enable you to change blades quickly and easily by hand. If not provided with the saw, they may be bought as an accessory.

· The **hold-down arm** has already been described on page 13. If your saw does not have one, consider buying it as an accessory.

· A **vacuum cleaner** is recommended to remove the dust created by cutting and sanding, which can be very harmful to lungs and eyes. Some scrollsaws have a built-in extraction port to which the vacuum cleaner can easily be attached. You can use an ordinary domestic vacuum cleaner or a purpose-made workshop one.

· **Lights and magnifiers** enhance your view of the pattern, making the lines easier to follow. There are many types available, some combining a light and a magnifier in one unit; we would recommend one of these, mounted on a universal clamp.

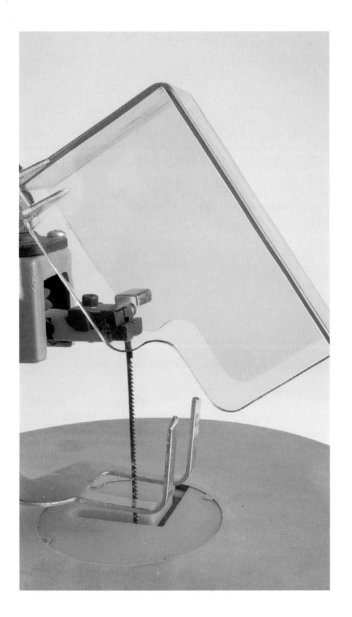

LEFT *This clear plastic blade guard provides protection without loss of visibility.*

Key point

In some of our pictures the blade guard has been removed to make it easier to photograph the work, but in normal use it should be left on whenever possible. Most guards nowadays are designed to permit good access and visibility.

· A **foot-activated power switch** gives you more control over the work because it leaves both hands free to stabilize and manoeuvre the wood. It allows you to pause in your work while you consider your cut line.

· Most modern machines have a clear plastic **blade guard** to help protect your fingers from accidental cuts. If your manufacturer has not provided one, it can be bought as an accessory.

· **Arm lifters** are spring-loaded or counterbalanced devices which serve to keep the upper arm of the scrollsaw raised when the blade is unclamped. They are not essential, but they do make it a little easier to rethread the blade when making inside cuts.

· A number of **sanding attachments** are available which can be fitted in place of the blade and used to sand the inner spaces of your project. An example is the Super Sander by Jim Dandy (see page 172), which is mounted on a rigid steel backing and comes in grades of 100 to 320 grit.

FOCUS ON:
Zero-clearance inserts

Most scrollsaw tables have a large hole in the centre where the blade passes through. This can be a nuisance when you are doing small-scale work, as the material close to the blade may not be adequately supported, so a replaceable insert is usually provided to plug the opening, leaving just enough clearance for the blade.

If your scrollsaw does not have such an insert, make a false table top by sawing into the centre of a piece of plywood and securing this to the saw table with two spring clamps. This will help stop small pieces from disappearing down the blade space, and reduce vibration when cutting thin wood. This simple device costs almost nothing to make, and is easily replaced when it becomes worn or damaged.

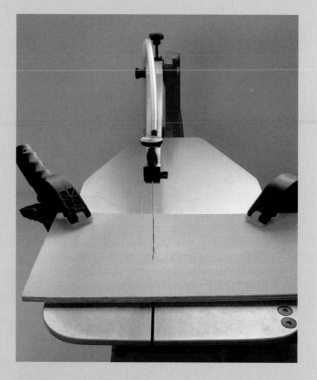

RIGHT *A false table top made from plywood, to support thin wood and stop small pieces disappearing down the blade opening, is attached to the scrollsaw table with spring clamps.*

Using the scrollsaw

The best way to learn is to practise. Draw straight and wavy lines on spare pieces of wood and practise cutting accurately on the lines. This will build up your confidence, provided you take your time and stay on the line!

Holding the workpiece with both hands, one either side of the blade, keeps you in control at all times. This is where the foot control comes into its own, as you do not have to take your hand off the work to stop the machine.

The general rule is to set the scrollsaw to a higher speed when cutting thicker material and a low speed for thin veneers and plywood. The rate at which you feed the wood through is very important: *do not force* the wood towards the blade, as this will cause premature wear and breakage. Work slowly with a gentle pressure, letting the saw do the work for you.

Adjust the hold-down arm so it applies just enough pressure to keep the wood stable while you are cutting.

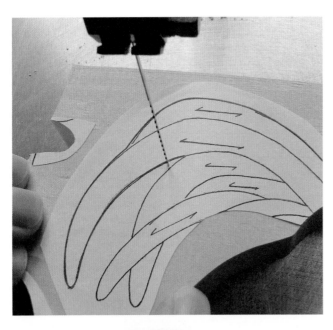

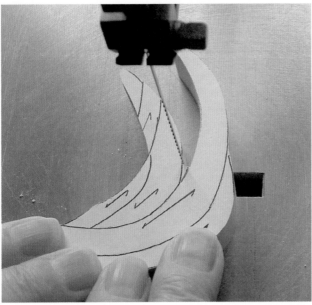

Technique

Although the scrollsaw is not especially good at cutting straight lines, you can clamp a temporary fence to the saw table to act as a guide.

ABOVE *The blade has been backed out of the apex of the V, and the workpiece turned round to enable the blade to cut back up the other side of the V.*

LEFT *Afterwards, a second cut removes the waste from the point of the V.*

Cutting technique

It's usually a good idea to cut the small pieces first, so you are left holding the largest, most manageable piece right up to the end. With some patterns this may mean sawing into the centre and then cutting the pieces from the inside out, as it were, numbering them as you go for easy reference.

Many patterns call for tight V-shapes to be cut, and there are two ways of handling this situation. One is to cut all the way into the V first and then back the blade out just enough to allow you to turn and continue along the cutting line. Alternatively, after cutting into the V, back the blade all the way out and then cut back into the V from a different direction to remove the waste. Practise both these methods and you will be able to deal with any situation.

To prevent overcutting as you come to the end of a line or are about to turn a corner, ease off the pressure just before you reach the turning point so the blade has time to catch up with you. With practice you should be able to make very clean corners in this way, which is one of the hallmarks of the experienced scrollsaw user.

Be patient and feed the work slowly, always letting the blade do the work, while you concentrate on the point of cut. Always try to cut exactly on the line, so eliminating it. Don't worry too much if you do go off the line – it is better to just follow through than try to correct it, as once the pattern is removed no one will know. The only time to be a little concerned is when you are making an inlay project where the pieces need to fit closely together; in this case the solution is to draw round the miscut piece as a template to cut out the adjoining piece, as shown over the page.

ABOVE *Forming a V-shape by making two cuts from opposite directions.*

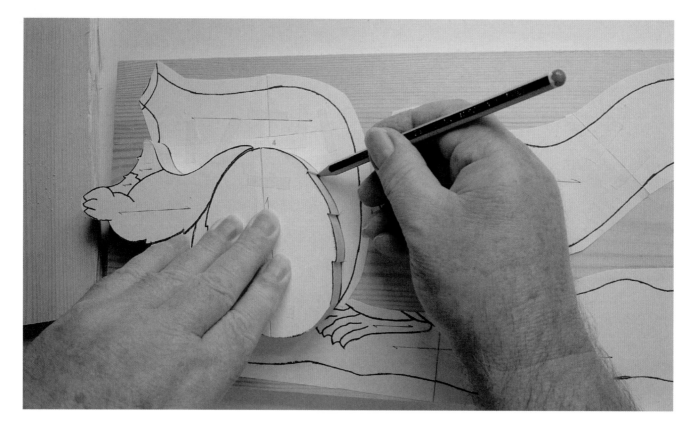

ABOVE *Using the first piece as a template to mark out the next.*

Ensuring an accurate fit

When you need to make a number of pieces that fit together, cut out one piece at a time, using each piece as a template to mark the next adjoining piece; this will keep unsightly gaps to a minimum.

Cutting internal openings

To make an enclosed cut, first drill a small hole just inside a corner or edge of the piece that is to be removed, then disconnect the top end of the blade, thread the blade through the hole, and reattach it to the scrollsaw in the usual way.

Stack-sawing

If you need to cut the same pattern in several pieces of thin wood, stack-cutting may be the answer. Simply stack the pieces one on top of the other and fasten them together with masking tape. Using the tape to hold all the outside edges together, make any internal cuts first, leaving the taped outside pieces till last. If the stack starts to separate, add more tape to secure the remaining pieces.

ABOVE *Threading the blade through a drilled hole in order to cut out an internal space.*

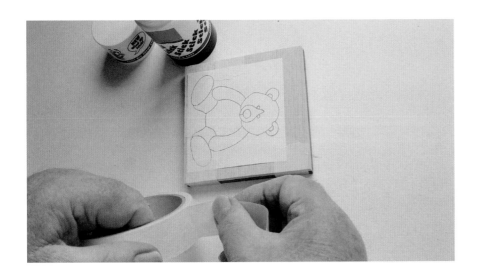

LEFT *Taping two layers of wood together to allow two pieces to be cut at the same time.*

FOCUS ON:

Troubleshooting

Ragged cut

This can be caused either by using a blade that is too coarse for the job, or one that has become dull. The answer is to change to either a new or a smaller blade.

Burning or scorching

If you find the wood is overheating as you cut, it could be that you are using too fine a blade at too fast a speed. Use slow speeds for small blades and faster speeds with the bigger blades. Another useful tip when cutting hardwood is to cover the wood or the pattern with clear packing tape; this helps to lubricate the blade, reducing burning to a minimum.

Blade will not cut easily

The most likely cause is a dull blade; change to a new one without delay. Continuing to use the saw with a dull blade causes unnecessary wear and tear on the machine, as well as inaccurate cutting.

ABOVE *The characteristic splintered or frayed edge left by a dull or excessively coarse blade.*

ABOVE *Scorched edges suggest that either the blade or the cutting speed you are using is inappropriate.*

Working with patterns

You will probably want to design your own projects eventually, but there are many published patterns available to get you started. Using published designs is a good way to get to know the scrollsaw and its capabilities before you strike out on your own.

Resizing the pattern

Practically all modern photocopiers have an enlargement and reduction facility, which offers an easy way to scale the pattern up or down to the required size for your project.

If you have access to the Internet and a flatbed scanner, there is an even easier alternative. Websites such as www.rapidresizer.com offer downloadable software, and a free trial is often available for a limited period. Scan the pattern into your computer, choose the size you want and then let the software do the rest.

Transferring the pattern to the work

The simplest method is to glue the pattern directly to the wood. First make enough copies to cover the different sections within the pattern (it's always a good idea to keep the original in case you need to make further copies), then lay these out and stick them to the wood using a glue stick (our preference) or spray adhesive. Alternatively, transferring the pattern using carbon paper gives you the added bonus of being able to see the grain of the wood. First trace the design on tracing paper, then position the tracing on the wood, moving it around until you feel that the lie of the grain suits the shape of each piece. When satisfied, slide the carbon paper underneath and go

Key point

Most published patterns, including those in this book, are protected by copyright. You may photocopy or scan the patterns in this book for your own private use, but they may not be reproduced for any other purpose without the written consent of the publisher and copyright owner.

LEFT *Gluing the patterns for the various sections to the wood. Notice how the arrows indicating grain direction are aligned with the grain of the wood, and the areas of awkward grain around the knots are avoided.*

over the tracing with a pencil or ballpoint to make a carbon copy on the wood. If tracing a large area, it's a good idea to tape down the corners of the tracing with masking tape – it can be most annoying to find you have accidentally moved the pattern halfway through the tracing process.

Removing the pattern

Both the glue stick and spray adhesives are quite low-tack, and if used sparingly should peel off relatively easily once the work is finished. For stubborn areas a light sanding with fine sandpaper usually does the job.

Creating your own designs

Start with something simple, such as a photograph or drawing of a favourite flower. Using tracing paper, trace around the main outline first, then add whatever other details you wish to include, such as the stem and a few leaves. Draw in some of the inner lines that make up the individual petals, leaf-veins, etc.; the experience you have gained by following the patterns in this book will help you to judge how easy or complex the pattern should be.

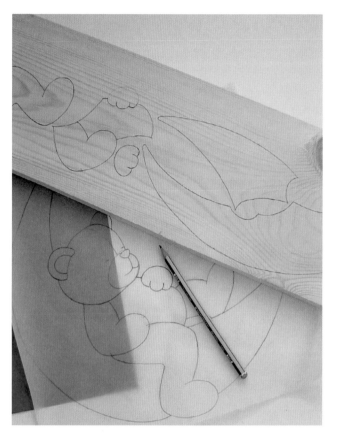

ABOVE *A pattern transferred using the more traditional method of tracing paper and carbon paper.*

Key point

No one can stop you deriving inspiration from other people's drawings or photographs, but if you imitate them too closely you may be in breach of copyright law, especially if you offer your work for sale. Try not to use other people's work as anything more than a springboard for your own creativity.

FOCUS ON:
Grain direction

For the sake of strength, the grain of the wood should normally run along the length of each component where possible, rather than across its width. For components of complex shape, it is usually best to align the grain with the narrowest or most fragile part of the outline. In our patterns we have used arrows where necessary to indicate the optimum grain direction.

Health and safety

It is extremely important that you take your own safety seriously while working with machinery, and are aware of how to use your saw properly; the scrollsaw is a safe tool as long as you are in control.

· Good ventilation is essential when working with tools that create dust, and a dust extractor is strongly recommended; a dust mask or respirator should be worn as well. Safety glasses or goggles are also essential for protecting your eyes from loose dust and small fragments of wood.

· Ear protection is always advisable when using machinery.

· Ensure that workplace lighting is adequate and can be adjusted as necessary.

· Be particular about disposing of shavings, finishing materials, oily rags, etc., which may be a fire hazard.

· Keep your hands clear of the blade and reciprocating arm of the scrollsaw at all times.

· Avoid loose clothing or jewellery which might catch in the blade, and if your hair is long, tie it back.

· Use hold-downs and safety guards whenever possible. The safety guards throughout the book have been removed for photographic purposes only.

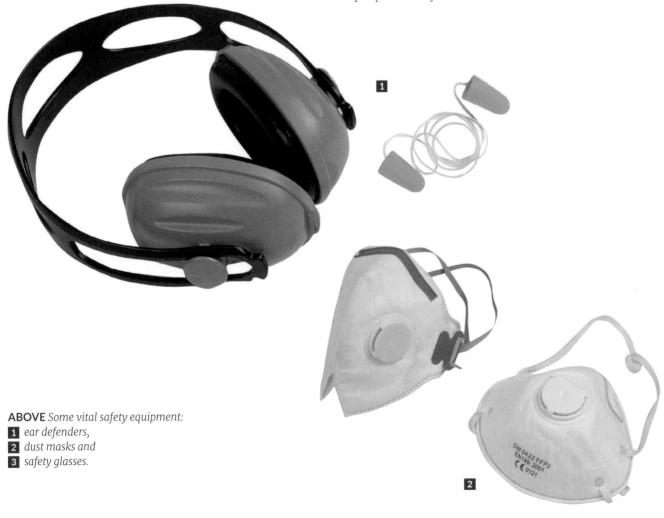

ABOVE *Some vital safety equipment:*
1 *ear defenders,*
2 *dust masks and*
3 *safety glasses.*

· Before switching on, ensure that the table is locked in position, the blade is as tight as it should be, and any adjusting keys have been removed.

· All scrollsaws are now fitted with a spring within the arm which prevents the top half of the blade falling out when it breaks, but be ready to stop the machine as soon as this happens.

· Do not force the work if the blade is not cutting easily, and stop if you smell burning (see 'Troubleshooting', page 23).

· If using a foot switch, make sure you cannot press it accidentally when changing the blade or making adjustments; it is best to unplug the machine or switch it off at the wall socket.

· Pay attention to electrical safety. Use correctly rated fuses in accordance with the manufacturer's instructions, and watch out for frayed leads. Do not allow leads to trail where you, or others, might trip over them.

· Prepare a first-aid kit suitable for treating cuts, scratches, friction burns and foreign objects in the eye; replace any items as soon as they are used.

· There is a slight risk of carpal tunnel syndrome if you press too hard on the work, and excessive vibration from an unbalanced machine can be harmful. Seek medical advice if you experience pain, numbness or tingling.

· Do not work when your concentration is impaired by drugs, alcohol or fatigue.

The safety advice in this book is intended for your guidance, but cannot cover every eventuality: the safe use of hand and power tools is the responsibility of the user. If you are unhappy with a particular technique or procedure, do not use it – there is always another way.

1:2
Other equipment & materials

Although the scrollsaw is a versatile tool, there are a number of other tools you will need to prepare the wood, mark out the design and bring the work to a good finish, and these are described on the following pages. Some are more important than others; many are familiar household or workshop items that you may already have.

This chapter also covers the raw materials that are used to make the projects in this book. The surface finish of your work is particularly important – it is the first thing your friends or customers will see – so we have devoted a special section to the materials used in colouring and finishing.

Additional tools

There are many tools which may be of use to the scrollsawer, but you will not need them all at the outset. Here are some of the tools we used to complete the projects in the book.

- **Disc sander** fitted with a 100-grit sanding disc. This is the ideal tool for rapid removal of unwanted wood, and we use it to make sure the wood is flat before we cut it. Even a slight bow in one component will make it out of square with the other pieces.

- **Drum sander** fitted into a variable-speed drill and supported in a drill stand. This is an invaluable tool when shaping curves. You must always sand with the grain to remove the scratches left by the disc sander.

- **Mini flexible-shaft tool** with an assortment of different-sized drums and sanding sleeves: useful for sanding small curves and shaping small areas of wood.

- **A pillar drill** allows you to be in control of the holes you need to drill. The wood can be safely clamped to the table of the pillar drill, and you can set the depth and angles with ease.

- A selection of **drill bits**, ranging in size from small wood drills (twist bits) to large 'flatbits'.

- A selection of **clamps**: spring clamps come in handy for securing the false plywood table described on page 19. Ordinary G-cramps (C-clamps) are always useful, too.

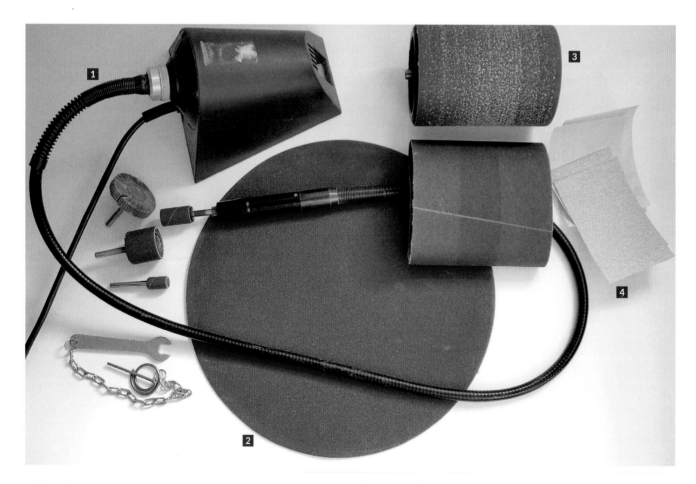

RIGHT *Sanding equipment:* **1** *flexible-shaft tool with sanding drums;* **2** *abrasive disc for a disc sander;* **3** *larger drums which can be attached to an electric drill mounted in a drill stand;* **4** *paper for hand-sanding.*

· A 6in (150mm) **try square** or an engineer's square is a must-have tool for checking the squareness of the blade in relation to the table, and for many other purposes.

· Other essential marking-out tools are a **ruler**, a **rectractable tape measure** and a **pencil** – always keep a pencil handy, especially for marking the top and bottom of your cut-out pieces.

· **Black marker pen**: used to mark the area on the backing where the wood will be glued, it provides good cover for any gaps that you may have, especially in those first few projects.

· **Wood burner**: this is not essential, but we use it to burn the eyes in certain projects; it seals the surface much better than an acrylic colour or wood stain, so the final gloss varnish has more lustre.

· **Pin hammer**: a small, lightweight hammer for driving in panel pins. Use it with a nail set to drive the pins below the wood surface.

· **Phillips screwdriver and screws** for attaching D-rings, etc.

· **Hand-sanding block** for sanding flat surfaces.

· A **buffing brush**, such as a shoe brush, for buffing up the surface after the polish has dried.

· **Artists' brushes** for applying paints, stains and varnishes.

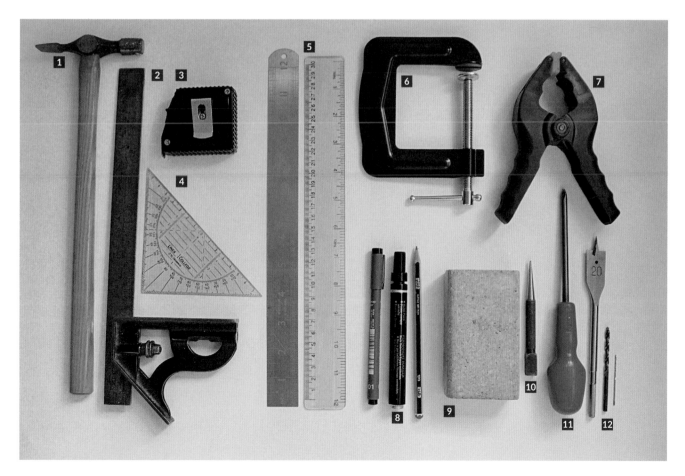

LEFT *Some indispensable hand tools:* **1** *pin hammer,* **2** *engineer's square,* **3** *tape measure,* **4** *set square or triangle,* **5** *rules,* **6** *G-cramp (C-clamp),* **7** *spring clamp,* **8** *pens and pencil,* **9** *cork sanding block,* **10** *nail set,* **11** *Phillips screwdriver,* **12** *flatbit and twist bits.*

Raw materials

ABOVE *Some of the materials required for the projects:* **1** *masking tape,* **2** *glue stick,* **3** *PVA wood glue,* **4** *tack cloth,* **5** *thin sheet of birch and mahogany,* **6** *various fixings,* **7** *lengths of dowel,* **8** *offcuts of pine and hardwood.*

The following materials will be needed to complete all the projects in the book:

· Pine is used in all of the projects, except for the trivets, for which hardwood is preferable. Pine is readily available and a renewable resource, which is environmentally friendly to our planet; and whenever possible we buy offcuts which have already been rejected for other uses. We would advise you to research any new woods you are thinking of using, perhaps by going online to one of the websites listed on page 172.

· ¼in (6mm) **birch plywood** is used to make backing pieces for many of the projects, and for three-dimensional constructions such as the bird house and utensil box.

· ⅛ and ¼in (3 and 6mm) **mahogany and birch sheets** are used to make the applied motifs which feature in many of the projects. These are readily available from craft supply stockists.

· **Hardwood dowels** will be needed in sizes from ⅛in (3mm) to ¾in (20mm).

· **Shaker pegs** are turned wooden pegs in a functional style, associated with the Shaker Christian communities. Reproductions are available from a number of specialist suppliers.

· Good-quality **wood glue** is needed for every project; we use PVA, both the ordinary and the weatherproof type.

· A **glue stick** of the kind used in offices is a convenient and easy way to attach paper patterns to wood, and much less messy than a spray adhesive. It allows the pattern to be peeled off reasonably easily when you have finished with it.

· Use **masking tape** to join together two or more pieces of wood for stack-sawing (see page 23).

· **Panel pins** will be needed for securing pieces of wood together in some of the projects.

· You will need an assortment of **sandpaper**, 120–320 grit – the coarser grades for shaping the wood, the finer grades for finishing.

· A resin-impregnated **tack cloth** is invaluable to remove fine dust before applying finish.

· Build up a selection of **acrylic paints, stains, mediums and varnishes** suitable for both interior and exterior use (more about this on the following pages).

· **Clear wax polish** adds that extra sheen to the finished project.

· **Soft, lint-free cloths** are always useful for polishing and for wiping off excess paint.

· Fixings for wall-hanging projects: our preferred options include **D-rings** screwed to the back of the work, or saw-tooth **picture hooks**; **mirror plates** provide a flush fixing and are extremely secure.

Colouring and finishing materials

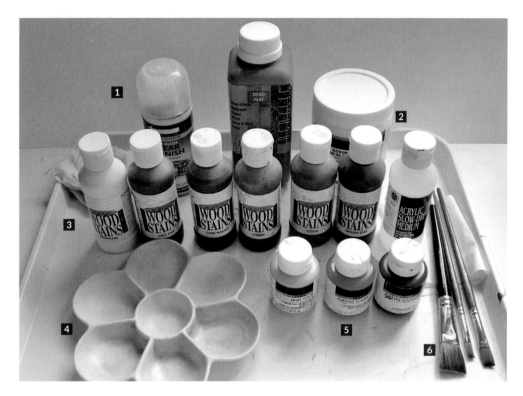

LEFT *Some of our preferred colouring materials:*
1 *acrylic varnish,*
2 *acrylic medium,*
3 *acrylic wood stains,*
4 *mixing palette,*
5 *artists' acrylic colours,*
6 *artists' brushes.*

The colouring and finishing of the project is just as important as the cutting, shaping and sanding. The time and care you have taken to cut the pieces out accurately will only be shown off at its best if the finishing is done with equal care.

Firstly you need to think about the kind of finish you would like: whether to use a translucent wood stain or opaque paint, for example. If you have used a nice piece of wood with attractive grain, we recommend that you highlight this instead of covering it up.

If you are unsure what colouring process to use, try them out on scraps of wood; this way you can see all the options available and decide which you prefer. This will also enable you to perfect your technique, ensuring your completed project has the finest finish possible.

Why we use acrylics

The range of colouring materials is very wide, including spirit-based, oil-based and water-based materials. There are many reasons why we prefer to use acrylic wood stains, paints and mediums:

· They don't give off fumes – unlike spirit stains, in particular, which can be used only in a well-ventilated room with no naked lights.

· Clean-up is easy with soap and water.

· They come in a wide range of vibrant colours which can easily be intermixed to create your own shades. Acrylic wood stains will bring out the natural beauty in all woods, even the cheaper ones such as pine.

· Spirit-based stains are far from easy to work with: they dry very fast because of their methylated spirit (denatured alcohol) content, and skill is needed to avoid overlaps. However, oil-based wood stains are easier to apply than spirit, and can give satisfactory results.

TECHNIQUE:
Applying wood stains

1 Brush on the acrylic stain; this is 'light oak'.

2 Use a soft cloth to remove the excess stain after a few moments.

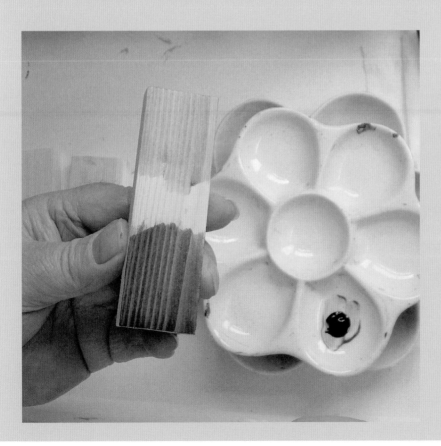

3 The 'medium walnut' stain in the foreground has been applied in the same way as the oak.

Using an acrylic medium

For most of our projects we use a medium in the colouring process. The purpose of this is to slow the drying of the acrylic paint, which gives you a longer working time. The amount of medium you add determines the translucency of the paint as well.

Our method is simple: we mix the medium with our chosen colours, paint onto the wood, leave for no longer than a minute, then wipe off the excess paint with a lint-free cloth to reveal the wood grain beneath without loss of colour.

Applying acrylic paint on its own to the wood surface would leave you with an opaque finish, whereas adding the slow-dry medium will thin the paint and at the same time enable you to remove the excess easily. The more pressure you apply when wiping the wood, the more grain you reveal. This will give each project uniqueness, as no two pieces of wood are the same. There is a whole range of mediums on the market, all made to do different jobs; for advice on which types to use, check out the websites of manufacturers such as Liquitex (see page 172).

Choosing varnishes for different finishes

Using varnish will achieve two things: it will protect your work and help to determine how your finished project looks. We use a matt varnish for most of the surface, and a high-gloss varnish to highlight certain areas such as the eyes. We also like to burn the eyes beforehand with a wood burner; this is not essential, but it seals the wood thoroughly, making a good base for the gloss varnish to adhere to, so improving the sparkle in the eye. Paying attention to small details like this really will enhance the overall appearance of the finished piece.

Polishing

If you want your finished project to feel as good as it looks, then a good wax polish is the answer. Once the varnish has finished drying, rub down the surface with a fine abrasive paper (around 320 grit) to remove any 'nibs' or specks; then apply a coat of clear wax polish with a soft cloth, and buff to a silky-smooth sheen with a buffing brush. Remember not to polish any areas where you have used a gloss varnish, otherwise you will lose that sparkle!

Wood fillers

Fillers can be used if necessary to repair cracks or holes in the wood, but try to avoid using them under a translucent finish, because they will not absorb the finish in the same way as the wood does. Fillers come in a range of colours to suit light, medium and dark woods. Use a flexible craft knife or palette knife to press the filler into the hole; when set hard, sand flush with the surface.

Wax sticks are also available in various wood shades and can be used to disguise small holes. Use a warm knife to soften the wax and press it into the hole; as the wax hardens, scrape it flush with the knife.

TECHNIQUE:
Applying acrylic paint

1 The red acrylic paint has been applied without any medium; when the excess is wiped off, the colour remains opaque.

2 Adding a little of the acrylic medium to the red.

3 This time, after wiping off the excess, the remaining colour is translucent and the wood grain underneath can be seen clearly.

2
Kitchen Projects

2:1
Maple-leaf trivets

Our kitchen projects explore a range of styles and techniques, and will give you plenty of practice in the basic skills of scrollsaw use. Since all of them are fairly straightforward, we have not graded them in order of difficulty – just choose those that appeal to you.

These attractive trivets are quite simple to make, and will be a great addition to your kitchen or dining table. We give two variations on the same design, which are effectively negatives of each other: one with the leaf veins left solid, and one with the veins cut out. Since they will be left in a natural state, an eye-catching hardwood will look best; in any case, the many sharp cross-grained projections would be very fragile in softwood. If you are new to scrollsawing, it is definitely worth practising these delicate cuts on a piece of scrap wood before you start on your chosen piece.

You will need:
· Hardwood of your choice, 10¼ x 8½ x ¾ in
  (260 x 215 x 19mm) for each trivet
· Scrollsaw and no. 7 blade
· Pillar drill and ⅛in (3mm) drill bit
· Photocopied patterns
· Scissors
· Glue stick
· Sanding block and sandpaper, 180–280 grit
· Tack cloth

Key point

Cutting these trivets from hardwood was a labour of love! Having a scrollsaw with variable speeds was definitely an asset, as cutting some hardwoods on a high speed can burn the wood badly and the burn marks are extremely hard to remove with hand-sanding alone. We would advise working on a fairly low speed – say 800–1000 strokes per minute, depending on your choice of wood – with an Olson no. 7 reverse-tooth blade, and cooling the blade with a fan if you have one handy, to keep the burn marks to a minimum. It may sound strange, but it does work.

Finished size: 9¹⁄₂ x 8in (240 x 200mm)
(This template needs to be enlarged to 122%)

Grain direction

Finished size: 9½ x 8in (240 x 200mm)
(This template needs to be enlarged to 122%)

Grain direction

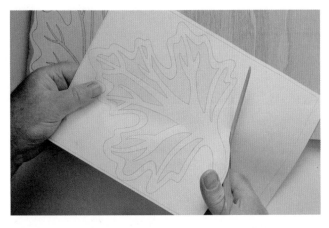

1 Photocopy each pattern to 9½ x 8in (240 x 200mm). The areas to be cut out are shaded to avoid confusion. Using scissors, cut around each leaf shape, leaving a border of, say, ³⁄₈in (10mm). Look at the direction of the wood grain and position each leaf with the stem in line with the grain, not across it. Apply an even coat with the glue stick over the whole area, then press firmly into place.

2 Fit the drill with the ¹⁄₈in (3mm) bit, and carefully drill a hole through each of the shaded areas to be cut.

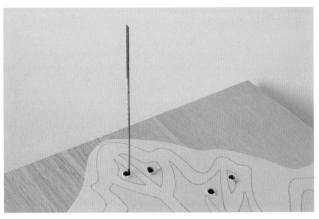

3 Pass the scrollsaw blade through the first hole, align and tighten the blade as described on page 17.

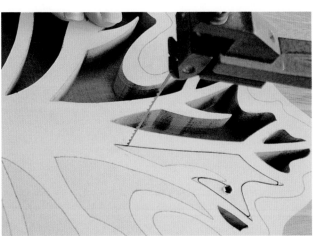

4 Proceed to cut out the first of the shaded areas, then each of the others in turn, rethreading and realigning the blade each time. With these tight corners, it's a good idea to cut into the V from one direction, then back the blade out just far enough to be able to turn and continue along the cutting line, then return to finish the cut once the majority of the waste has been removed.

5 The cut-out areas in the second design are much narrower, but the technique is the same. Work carefully and do not rush.

6 With all the shaded areas cut out and removed from both trivets, cut around the outer edge of each maple leaf to remove the waste.

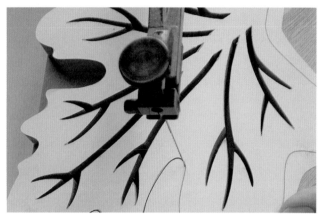

7 Remove the pattern; using a damp cloth to moisten the paper will help you to lift the pattern easily from the wood.

8 When dry, use a sanding block fitted with 180-grit sandpaper to remove any residue left by the glue, then hand-sand around the edges to remove the burr. Lastly, wipe the trivets with a tack cloth to remove the fine dust. You can leave the hardwood trivets in their natural state.

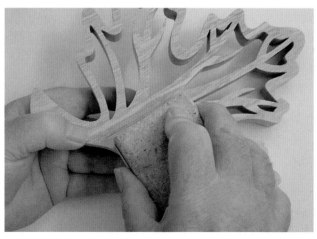

2:2
Poppy utensil box

This simple wall-hanging holder for wooden spoons, spatulas and the like is easy to make and will be an attractive and practical addition to your kitchen. We have included a daisy motif as an alternative to the poppies, so you could match the design to the decor of your own kitchen. You could even use a motif from elsewhere in the book if you prefer.

You will need:
- ¼in (6mm) birch plywood, 24 x 10in (610 x 254mm)
- ⅛in (3mm) sheet birchwood, 5¼ x 4in (134 x 102mm)
- ³/₁₆in (5mm) hardwood beading, 15¾in (400mm) long
- Scrollsaw with no. 1 and no. 5 blades
- Pillar drill and ¼in (6mm) drill bit
- Clamps as needed
- Masking tape
- Sanding block and sandpaper, 180–320 grit
- Tack cloth
- Photocopied patterns
- Scissors
- Pencil
- Ruler
- PVA wood glue
- Glue stick
- Acrylic paint: green, red and black
- Artists' brushes
- Soft lint-free cloth
- Acrylic matt varnish

Key point

The finger joints in this project need to fit accurately, but don't be put off by this – it is not as difficult as it looks. Once you have sawn the cut-outs, you may need to go back to the saw a second time to tidy the corners and make sure they are square. Then check the fit, and carefully pare away any high spots. Crisply cut finger joints can be a decorative feature in their own right.

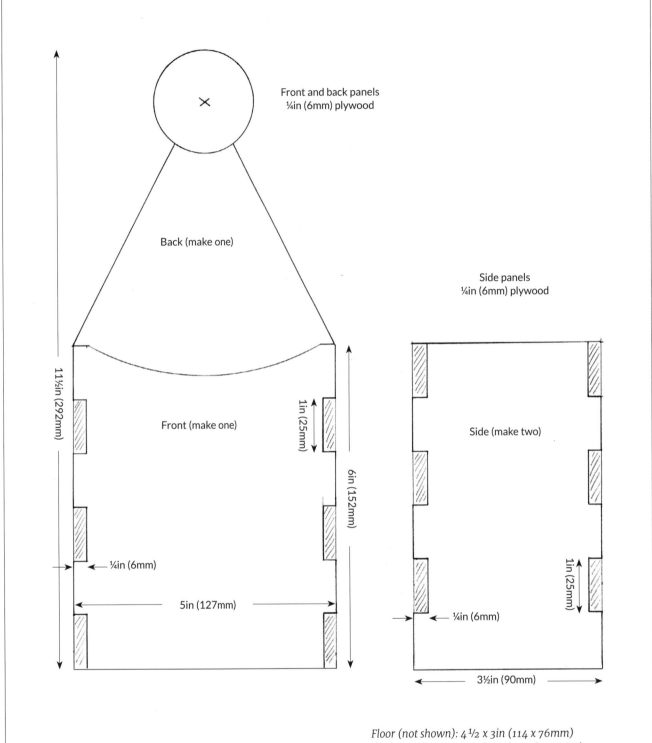

Front and back panels
¼in (6mm) plywood

Back (make one)

Side panels
¼in (6mm) plywood

Front (make one)

Side (make two)

11½in (292mm)

1in (25mm)

6in (152mm)

¼in (6mm)

5in (127mm)

1in (25mm)

¼in (6mm)

3½in (90mm)

Floor (not shown): 4 ½ x 3in (114 x 76mm)
(This template needs to be enlarged to 176%)

LEFT *Poppy motif*
Finished size: 5 x 3in (127 x 76mm)

ABOVE *Alternative daisy motif*
Finished size: 5 x 4in (127 x 102mm)

(These templates are shown at actual size)

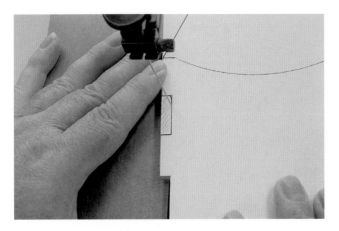

1 Enlarge the two box patterns to the sizes given. Cut the plywood into four equal parts of 12 x 5in (305 x 127mm) each. Stack these in pairs – one pair for the front and back sections, the other for the two sides – and tape them together. Attach the two patterns to the plywood surfaces with the glue stick. Cut out the panels, making the finger joints as square and as accurate as you can.

2 Remove the masking tape to separate the pieces. At this stage the front panel is the same shape as the back, so you must now cut off the unwanted top part from the front panel. Fit a drill (preferably a pillar drill) with a ¼in (6mm) drill bit and drill the hole in the top section of the back panel for hanging up the utensil box. Cut the base from the remaining piece of plywood.

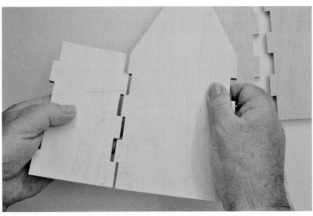

3 Peel off the patterns and check to see that the panels all fit together properly; mark any high spots in pencil and cut off thin slivers where necessary. Do not glue anything at this stage. Brush away the dust and then wipe over with a tack cloth to remove any fine dust that remains. Using an artist's brush, apply an acrylic matt varnish to all the surfaces except for the areas to be glued, and allow to dry thoroughly. Lightly sand the panels with 220-grit sandpaper on a sanding block.

4 Photocopy the poppy pattern and attach it to the sheet of birchwood using the glue stick, pressing firmly so that the entire pattern is well stuck down. Fit a no. 1 blade and set the scrollsaw to a slow speed, say 400–600 strokes per minute. Cut out the poppy, saving the waste as a template for use later. When finished, peel off the pattern; if it is stubborn, dampen with a cloth and carefully scrape away the paper with a small craft knife.

5 You could paint the poppy as it is now, but cutting out the individual pieces will give an enhanced appearance of relief. If your saw does not have a zero-clearance insert, you would be wise to make one as described on page 19, so the small pieces will not disappear down the centre hole. As you cut each piece out, mark the underside to avoid confusion. Very lightly sand the edges with 320-grit paper, then remove any fine dust with a tack cloth.

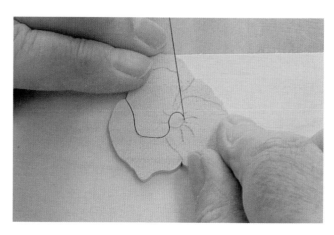

6 Sort the pieces into colour groups, then, using an artist's brush, mix together each of the paints and mediums as described on page 36, and apply the paint. Allow to dry completely, then lightly rub down with 320-grit sandpaper, as the painting process may have raised the grain of the wood. Wipe away the fine dust with the tack cloth, then apply a coat of acrylic matt varnish, and leave to dry.

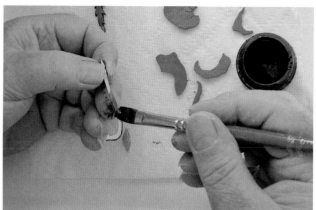

7 Lay the front panel of the box on a flat surface, position the template (the waste material saved from cutting out the poppy) onto the centre and secure with masking tape. Now apply a dab of PVA glue to the underside of each piece in turn and glue in position. When finished, carefully lift off the template and remove any excess glue with a small damp cloth or old artist's brush, and allow to dry.

8 Lay out the box panels in order for gluing, apply PVA glue where the joints meet together, then clamp securely until dry. When the sides are dry, glue the small beading strips onto the inside bottom edge of the box, so the floor of the box rests on the beading, making it easy to remove for cleaning purposes.

Now you can place your utensils in the box and either hang it on the wall or leave it free-standing.

2:3
Daisy doorstop

Most doorstops are purely functional items, but there is no reason why they should not be made attractive as well, and this daisy design will certainly not go unnoticed. We have included a poppy design as an alternative to the daisies. Alternatively, you could make a mixture of both types of flower and display them in a vase.

You will need:
- Hardwood for the wedge, 7 x 1¾ x 1in (178 x 44 x 25mm)
- Small piece of pine for the daisies, 12 x 4 x ¾ in (305 x 102 x 19mm)
- ¼in (6mm) hardwood dowel, 24in (610mm) long
- Scrollsaw and no. 7 blade
- Disc sander
- Drum and mini flexible-shaft sanders, with selection of sanding sleeves
- Sanding block and sandpaper, 120–320 grit
- Pillar drill and ¼in (6mm) drill bit
- Photocopied patterns
- Scissors
- Masking tape
- Cling film (plastic food wrap)
- Pencil
- Ruler
- Good-quality wood glue
- Glue stick
- Acrylic paints: white, yellow and green
- Acrylic matt vanish
- Artists' brushes
- Wax polish and soft polishing cloth
- Tack cloth

For safety:

- Understand your tools and machinery; always read the manufacturer's instructions.
- Eye and ear protection are essential.
- Dust can also be a hazard to your health: wear a dust mask or respirator. Investing in a dust extractor or some form of vacuum cleaner is also a good idea.

Central daisy head and back support

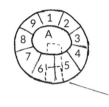

Stem length: 9in (230mm)

Drilled hole ¼in (6mm) dia., ½in (13mm) deep

Left daisy head and back support

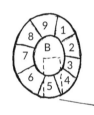

Stem length: 8in (200mm)

Drilled hole ¼in (6mm) dia., ½in (13mm) deep

Right daisy head and back support

Stem length: 7in (178mm)

Drilled hole ¼in (6mm) dia., ½in (13mm) deep

⟶ *Grain direction*

– – – – – – – *Position of stem*

(Daisy templates need to be enlarged to 125%)

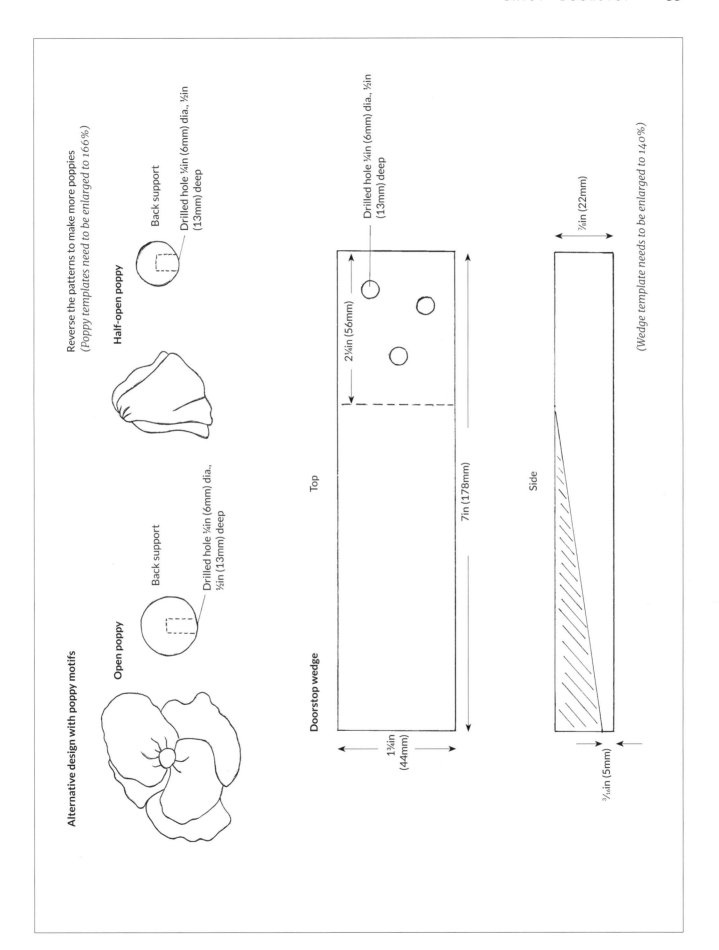

Alternative design with poppy motifs

Reverse the patterns to make more poppies
(*Poppy templates need to be enlarged to 166%*)

Open poppy

Half-open poppy

Back support

Drilled hole ¼in (6mm) dia., ½in (13mm) deep

Back support

Drilled hole ¼in (6mm) dia., ½in (13mm) deep

Doorstop wedge

Top

Drilled hole ¼in (6mm) dia., ½in (13mm) deep

2¼in (56mm)

7in (178mm)

1¾in (44mm)

Side

⅞in (22mm)

(*Wedge template needs to be enlarged to 140%*)

³⁄₁₆in (5mm)

1 Each flower has a supporting piece at the back to which the petals and centre are glued. Start by making a photocopy of each back support, and two copies of each daisy-head pattern. Note how the grain runs approximately along the length of each petal. For the first (central) daisy, cut one of the patterns so you have three petals at the top (petals 9, 1, 2), the flower centre, and two petals at the bottom (5, 6); cut the second pattern to give the remaining petals on either side (3, 4, 8, 7). Align the petals with the wood grain, then glue-stick the patterns to the wood. Do the same for the other daisies.

2 Set up the scrollsaw with a no. 7 blade. Cut the main part of the daisy first, leaving the petals attached to the centre for the moment. Cut into the V-shape between the petals, then back the blade out just enough to turn the work round to cut the next petal.

3 Return afterwards to remove the waste. Keep a piece of 180-grit sandpaper handy to remove the burr from the underside of the cut line as you go.

4 Place this centre piece over the side petals to check that the shape still matches; if you have wandered from the line, trace the shape onto the next piece to be cut, then cut this piece following your new line. When you have cut the pieces out, check that they fit well together.

5 Now cut out the individual petals. Before you remove the pattern, number each petal on the underside, quite close to where they meet the centre, so the numbers will be hidden once the back support is glued on. Also mark the position of the first petal on the centre piece. Cut out the other two daisies in the same way; it's a good idea to label them straight away, and keep the three sets of petals separate!

6 Cut out the three back supports, leaving the patterns in place until it is time to glue. Cut the dowel for the stems to 9, 8 and 7in (230, 200 and 180mm). Fit the pillar drill with a ¼in (6mm) bit. Use a clamp to hold the back support so that the drill lines up with the appropriate mark on the pattern and is set back approximately ¼in (6mm) from the face of the pattern. Holding the clamp securely, carefully drill down ½in (13mm).

7 Using the disc sander, taper each petal down by ¹⁄₁₆ or ⅛in (2 or 3mm) towards the centre of the flower. Round over the three back supports as best you can, leaving the pattern attached; then move on to the drum sander to round them further.

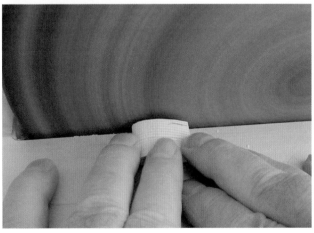

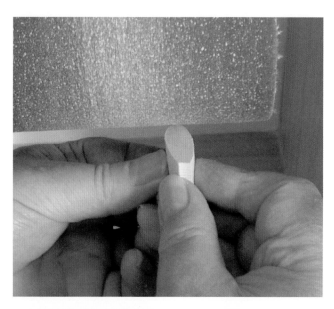

8 Also use the drum sander to round over the petals, always sanding with the grain.

9 Mark the height of each petal onto the centre piece, then round over the centre piece to this line. Hand-sand all the pieces to a smooth finish with 180-grit through to 280-grit sandpaper, and then wipe all the pieces with a tack cloth to remove the fine dust before colouring.

10 Still keeping each daisy separated, sort the pieces into small groups for colouring. The paints are mixed with medium as described on page 36. Paint the front, sides and the exposed part of the back of each petal, then wipe off the excess with a soft cloth to reveal the grain. Paint the centres a bright yellow and use green mixed with medium for the back supports and stems. Allow to dry, preferably overnight. Lightly nib down the pieces with 320-grit sandpaper, again remove the fine dust with a tack cloth, then varnish all the pieces and leave to dry. Polish (we used Liberon Black Bison neutral) and buff to a nice sheen.

11 Tape a piece of cling film (food wrap) to the work surface to stop the flower heads sticking. Referring to the numbers on the underside, arrange the petals in order around the centre pieces. Glue the petals one at a time, firmly pressing them into place. If any glue has seeped out, wipe away with a damp cloth and an old acrylic artist's brush. Glue all three flower heads, and leave to dry on the cling film.

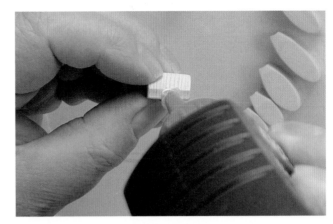

12 When dry, attach the correct back support to each flower head, aligning the pre-drilled hole to the correct petal number as shown on the drawing. Apply a dab of glue, press firmly into place and leave to dry thoroughly.

13 Any available hardwood can be used for the wedge. Make a copy of the pattern top and attach it to the wood using the glue stick. Use the same bit as before to drill the stem holes. The centre hole is vertical; the other two are slanted outwards by placing a small piece of ¼in (6mm) plywood under the side of the wedge before drilling. Wetting the paper with a damp cloth will help the pattern to peel off.

14 Mark the wedge shape with a ruler and pencil, then remove the waste with the scrollsaw. Sand the wedge smooth with a sanding block and 120-grit sandpaper, then use 280-grit paper for an all-over smooth finish. Wipe with a tack cloth, varnish with an acrylic matt varnish, and allow to dry. Polish will give the wedge a nice sheen. To assemble, just push the three stems into their respective holes.

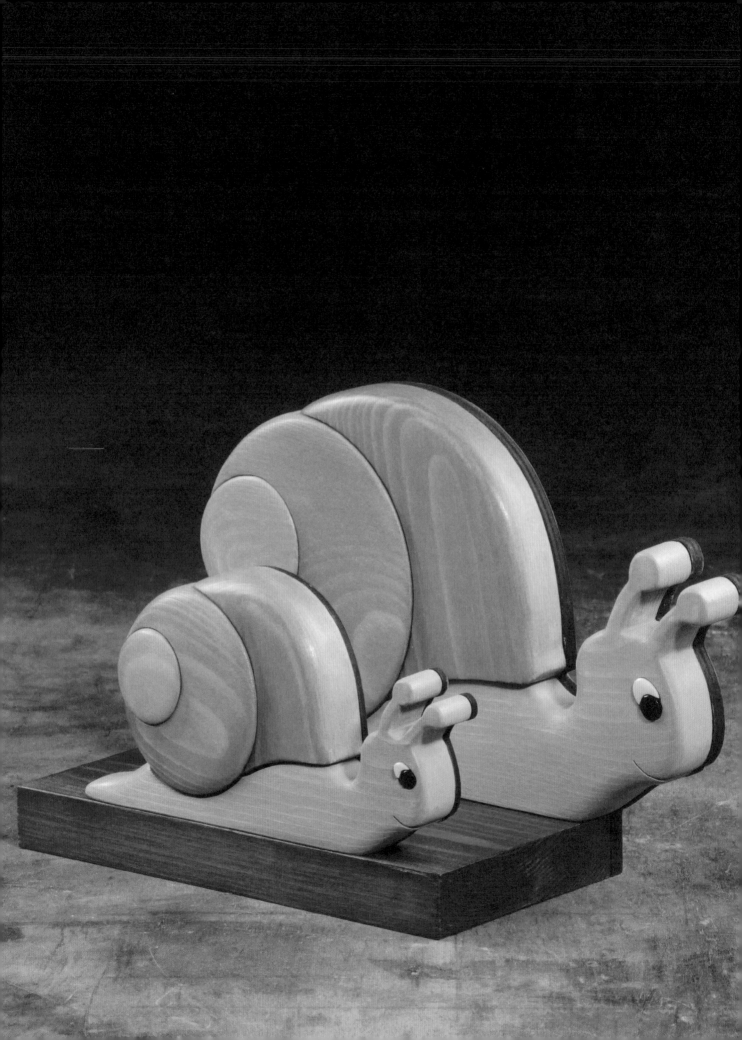

2:4
Snail-mail letter rack

Keep track of your snail mail with this cheeky pair of molluscs. The two gastropods are an exact match because they are made to the same pattern, enlarged for one and reduced for the other. If you prefer, you could make just the one snail and use it as a wall decoration.

You will need:
- Pine, 24 x 6 x ¾in (610 x 152 x 19mm)
- ¼in (6mm) plywood, 10 x 6in (254 x 152mm)
- ⅛in (3mm) plywood, 5½ x 3¼in (140 x 82mm)
- Very short offcuts of ¼in (6mm) and ⁵/₁₆in (8mm) hardwood dowel
- Scrollsaw with no. 7 and no. 1 blades
- Disc sander
- Drum and mini flexible-shaft sanders, with a selection of sanding sleeves
- Sanding block and selection of sandpaper, 120–320 grit
- Pillar drill with ¼ and ⁵/₁₆in (6 and 8mm) bits
- Photocopied patterns
- Scissors
- Masking tape
- Pencil
- Ruler
- PVA wood glue
- Glue stick
- Acrylic paints: white, green and black
- Acrylic medium
- Acrylic wood stains: light oak and medium oak
- Acrylic matt and gloss varnish
- Acrylic sanding sealer
- Artists' brushes
- Wood burner
- Wax polish and soft polishing cloth
- Tack cloth
- D-ring
- Small screw

Key point

Don't overlook the creative possibilities of the photocopier! Enlarging or reducing the same pattern to different sizes is a very easy way to make your designs go further. Also, if you draw your patterns on tracing paper, you can photocopy them from both sides to create mirror-image versions. This gives you several different designs for the price of one.

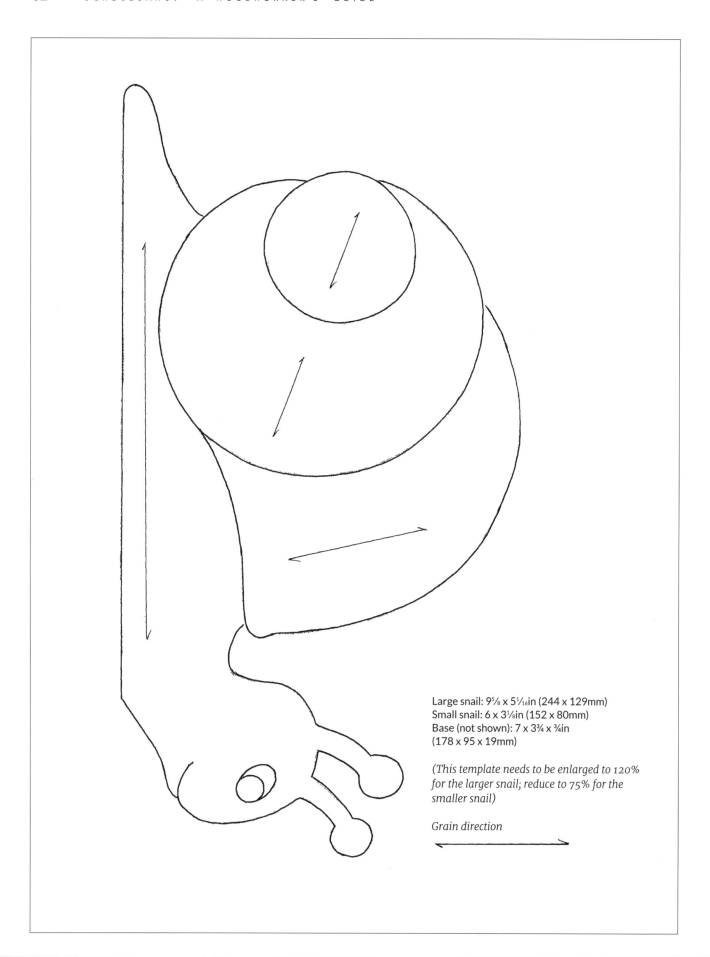

Large snail: 9⅝ x 5¹/₁₆in (244 x 129mm)
Small snail: 6 x 3⅛in (152 x 80mm)
Base (not shown): 7 x 3¾ x ¾in
(178 x 95 x 19mm)

*(This template needs to be enlarged to 120%
for the larger snail; reduce to 75% for the
smaller snail)*

Grain direction

1 Make three copies of the pattern in each of the two sizes. Cut out three separate patterns for each snail – body, outer shell and inner shell – with approximately $^3/_8$in (10mm) border around each. Lay the patterns out on the wood, matching the wood grain with the directional arrows on the patterns, and attach with a glue stick.

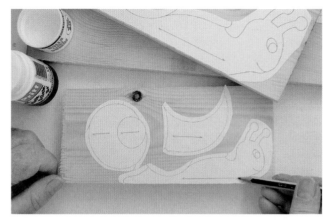

2 Fit the pillar drill with the $^5/_{16}$in (8mm) bit, align the larger of the two snail bodies and clamp securely in place, then drill the hole for the eye, which goes all the way through. Change to the $^1/_4$in (6mm) bit and drill the eye hole for the smaller snail.

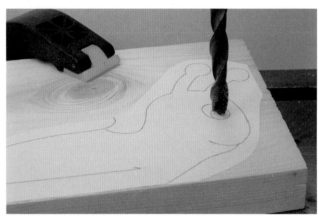

3 Fit a no. 7 blade to the scrollsaw, check the alignment and tighten as described on page 17. Cut the outer (right-hand) shell piece first; have a piece of 180-grit sandpaper handy to remove the burr from each piece you cut.

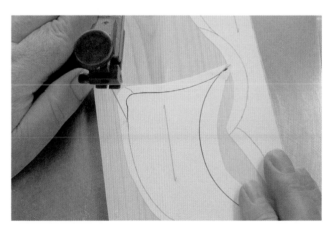

4 Lay this piece over the main circular part of the shell; if it does not match, run a sharp pencil around it to correct the outline of the next piece.

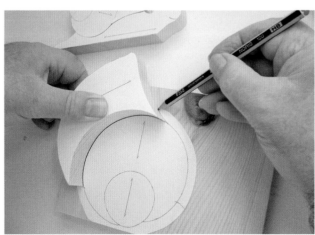

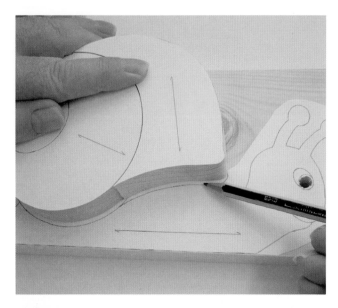

5 Cut out the main circular part of the shell, then cut out the small inner circle, as seen on the workbench in photo 7 below. Align both sections of the shell on the body of the snail, trace the shape as before, and then cut out the snail body.

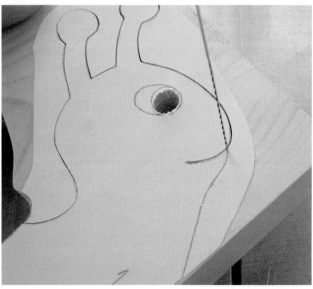

6 When you reach the mouth, cut all the way in, then back the blade out and continue to cut the outline of the throat.

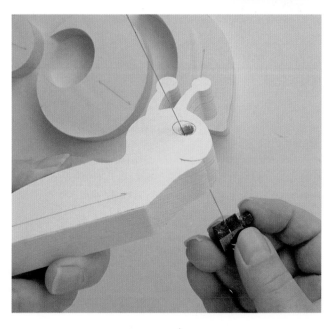

7 To cut out the white section of the eye, release the tension on the scrollsaw and undo one end of the blade from its clamp, then pass the blade through your pre-drilled hole and reattach the blade in the usual way. Set the scrollsaw at a lower speed, say 600 strokes per minute, and carefully cut out this small piece.

Mark the underside of each piece so you know which side to sand; also mark a pencil line down the edges where one piece meets another, and be mindful of these areas when sanding.

8 Use the disc sander to create different levels of relief. Thin down the body by ¹⁄₈in or so (3mm) at the head end and a fraction more towards the tail. Next sand the outer shell piece down by ¹⁄₈in (3mm), then reduce the larger circle by ¹⁄₁₆in (2mm), leaving the small inner circle untouched. Now you can see your snail already beginning to take on a three-dimensional appearance.

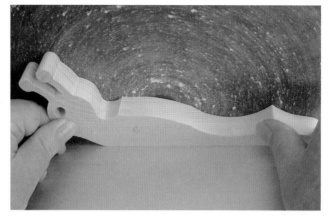

9 Using the drum and flexible-shaft sanders to round over and smooth the pieces will make the snail look even better. Start with the tail section on the drum sander.

10 Then use the smaller flexible-shaft tool to sand around the small curves near the head.

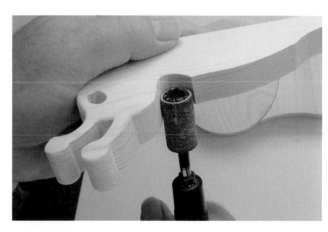

11 As each piece is shaped, mark the thickness of it onto the adjoining piece and do not sand below this mark. Do not sand the inside edge of the outer shell where it meets the main circular part, or the inside edge of the main part where it meets the smaller circle. The small circle will only need a little sanding, as this is the highest piece.

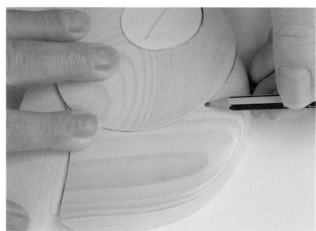

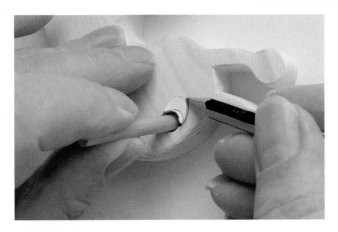

12 Mark the height of the head on the piece that will be the white of the eye (a small dowel helps to hold this in position while you do so) and on the offcut of dowel that will be the pupil. Sand and round these eye pieces to just above the pencil line. Hand-sand all the pieces to a smooth finish, using 180-grit paper, then 220-grit. Dust with a soft brush, then wipe away the fine dust with a tack cloth.

13 Burn the top of each dowel with a wood burner; this will seal the end grain of the dowel, giving the gloss varnish a better finish.

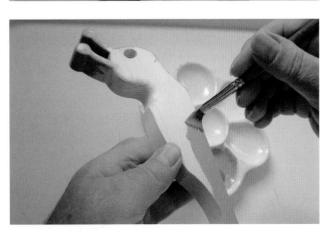

14 When both snails are fully shaped, sort the pieces for colouring: we used white for the white of the eye, Baltic green for the snail body and light oak wood stain for the shell. Mix the paint with medium and apply with an artist's brush and wait.

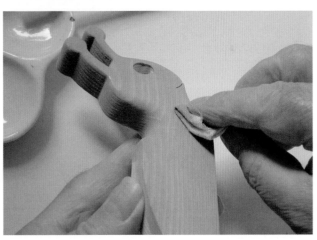

15 Wipe off the excess with a soft cloth to reveal the grain. When completely dry, lightly rub down all the pieces with 320-grit sandpaper, then wipe away the fine dust with a tack cloth. Apply acrylic gloss varnish to the eyes and matt varnish to everything else, then leave to dry. Again lightly rub down and wipe with the tack cloth. Apply a coat of polish to all surfaces except the eyes, then buff to a nice sheen.

16 To make the backing pieces, first assemble the small snail onto the thinner piece of plywood and the large snail on the thicker piece. Use a sharp pencil to trace around each snail, leaving an extra ¾ in (19mm) at the bottom of the larger snail to glue the base onto. Our base is pine, 7 x 3¾ x ¾ in (178 x 95 x 19mm), stained with a medium oak acrylic wood stain and varnished.

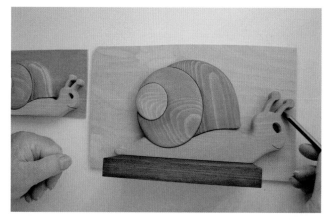

17 Also trace around the main shell pieces. Cut out the plywood backing pieces, using a no. 1 blade for the thinner piece and no. 5 for the thicker piece, then draw over the outlines of the individual pieces with a thick black marker pen; darkening the background in this way will help to disguise any gaps between the pieces. Apply a sanding sealer to the back of the plywood; when dry, paint the edges matt black to make them look neat.

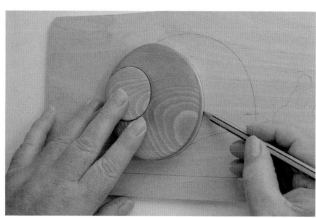

18 Glue the snail pieces one at a time onto their respective backing pieces, then set them aside to dry.

19 Apply glue to the underside of the large snail and the extended plywood backing, position onto the base and secure with two clamps until dry. Glue the small snail centrally onto the front of the base, and again leave to dry. The photograph shows the neat appearance of the finished letter rack from the back.

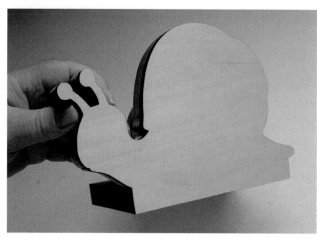

Cockerel chalkboard

Never forget again, with this colourful kitchen noticeboard! We have placed the cockerel motif on the left-hand side of the board, but if you are left-handed you may prefer to reverse the pattern and put him on the right.

You will need:

- Planed pine: about 16 x 7 x ¾ in (400 x 170 x 20mm) will be ample
- ¼ in (6mm) MDF (medium-density fibreboard), 21¾ x 16in (550 x 400mm)
- Softwood or hardwood strip: two pieces 11 x ½ x ¼ in (280 x 13 x 6mm)
- Scrollsaw and no. 7 blade
- Disc sander
- Drum sander
- Flexible-shaft tool with rubber-drum sanding kit
- Bradawl
- Screwdriver
- Wood burner
- Photocopied patterns
- Pencil
- Sanding block and sandpaper, 120–320 grit
- Artists' brushes
- 1in (25mm) paintbrush
- Matt black (chalkboard) paint
- Acrylic paints: yellow, red, parchment, blue, green
- Acrylic wood stains: light oak, cherry, cedar
- Slow-dry acrylic medium
- Acrylic matt or satin varnish
- Soft cloth
- PVA wood glue
- Spray-mount adhesive
- Tack cloth
- Permanent black marker pens: thick and fine
- Two D-rings
- Two small screws
- Picture wire or string

For safety:

- Understand your tools and machinery; always read your power-tool instructions.
- Eye and ear protection are essential.
- Dust can be a health hazard: wear a dust mask or respirator. Investing in a dust extractor or some form of vacuum is always a good idea.

Colour guide
Beak and ear: parchment
Feet: light oak stain
Breast and hocks: cherry stain
Comb and wattles: red
Neck: yellow
Tail: green
Saddle (back): blue
Wing: cedar stain

Finished size: 8 ¾ x 6 ¾ in (220 x 170mm)
(This template needs to be enlarged to 117%)

Grain direction

1 Print off five copies of the cockerel pattern, then cut out the nine sections of the pattern with scissors, leaving a narrow border around each. Spray-mount each section on the wood, aligning the arrows with the wood grain and avoiding any knots; press down firmly onto the wood and allow to dry.

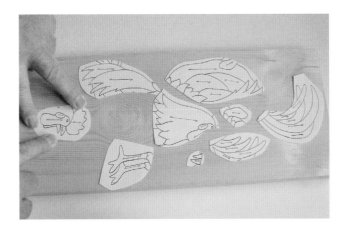

2 Drill the eye with a $\frac{1}{8}$in (3mm) bit.

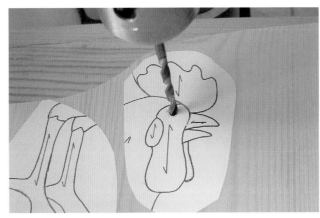

3 Align the scrollsaw blade straight and taut, and cut out all the sections of the pattern. To cut the zigzag outline of the saddle (the feathers on the cock's back), first cut all the way down one side of the V, then back the blade all the way out and cut in from the other side to remove the waste material.

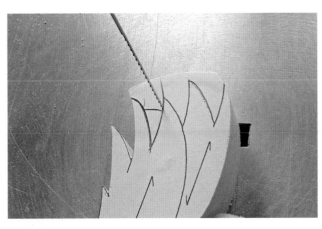

4 An alternative method, shown here on the tail feathers, is to cut into the angle from one side, then back the blade out just enough to turn the workpiece and continue cutting.

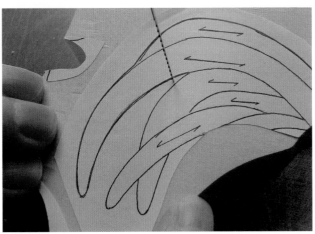

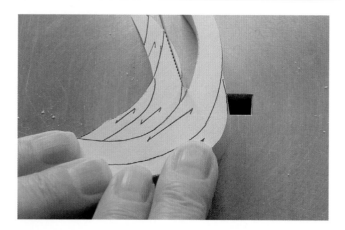

5 Return afterwards to remove the waste.

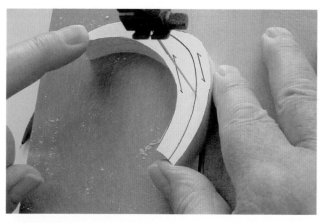

6 You should now have a total of 13 sections cut out; arrange them together to check the fit. Now you can proceed to cut out the individual pieces, including the two sections of the beak.

7 Number each of the tail feathers on the underside, as shown on the pattern, as you cut each separate piece. Mark all the other pieces on the underside (we used B for 'bottom') so you can see which side to sand. It is also helpful to mark a line along the edge where one piece meets another, for easy location later.

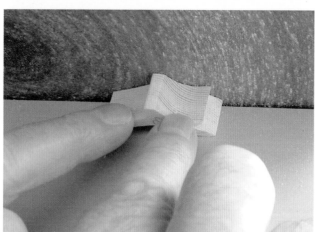

8 Use the disc sander to create the different levels of relief, which will begin to give the cockerel a three-dimensional appearance. Start by reducing the thickness of the right foot down to about 5/8in (15mm), then make the left foot a trifle thicker than this.

9 Mark the height of the right foot onto the right hock (the upper part of the leg), and sand down the hock to just above this line. Proceed in the same way, marking the height of the hock on the lower edge of the breast and sanding the breast down to the pencil line but not beyond.

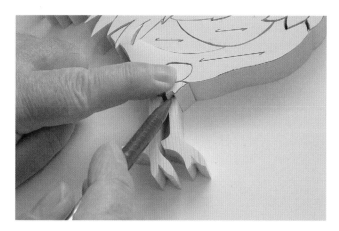

10 The small fragment of breast that shows between the saddle feathers must match the height of the main breast section, to give the illusion of one continuous surface. Mark the height of the breast pieces onto the three wing pieces; these are sanded only just enough to remove the paper pattern.

11 Begin to shape the tail on the disc sander by lowering feathers 4 and 5 to about ⅝in (15mm) thick. Mark the height of these two pieces onto the adjoining feathers 3 and 6, and reduce no. 3 to just above this line. Mark the height of this piece onto no. 2 and sand that to just above the line. Repeat the process with no. 1. Nos. 7 and 6 are tapered in thickness, being thinner where they join the back.

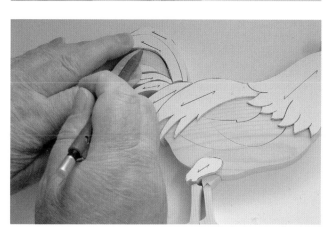

12 Mark the heights of the tail pieces onto the smaller back (saddle) piece and sand this to just above the mark. Repeat with the larger saddle piece, then mark the height of the body pieces on the neck. Sand the neck, face and comb pieces on the drum sander just enough to remove the pattern; the beak can be taken a little lower. Lastly, mark the height of all the pieces around the left hock and sand to just above the line.

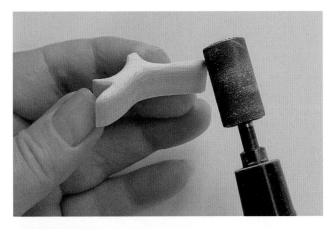

13 The drum sander and the flexible-shaft machine are great for rounding over all the edges, small and large. Start with the lowest level – the feet – then move on to the tail pieces, using the flexible shaft to round the smaller curves. Round the breast all along the outer edge, and shape the small breast piece to match. Lightly smooth the wing and saddle pieces.

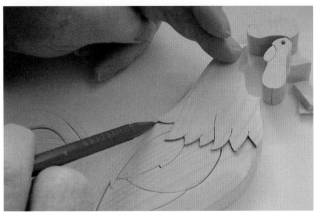

14 Using a pencil, re-mark the now rounded body pieces onto the neck piece and sand this to the line. The wattle (cheek) pieces need only a little sanding to smooth the edges; the smaller piece is sanded a little lower, so it appears further away. Sand the edges of the beak pieces smooth. Hand-sand all the pieces to a smooth finish, using first 180-grit and then 220-grit sandpaper.

15 Roll up a small piece of 280-grit sandpaper and clean out the drilled hole to take the eye. Cut the dowel to length and round off the end with 280-grit sandpaper. Use a wood burner to seal the end of the dowel, then apply satin varnish with a soft brush and allow to dry.

16 Mixing the paints and stains with a slow-dry medium will allow you a longer working time. Each colour is brushed on and left for a moment, then the surplus is wiped off with a soft, lint-free cloth. Give the pieces a slight rub-down with 280-grit sandpaper, wipe over with a tack cloth to remove any fine dust, and apply an acrylic matt or satin varnish, wiping off any surplus. Allow to dry thoroughly.

17 Measure out an 18 x 12in (460 x 305mm) oblong in the bottom right-hand corner of your MDF. Assemble the cockerel onto the board so the head and tail sit just outside the top left-hand corner of this rectangle, and draw around the shape of the bird with a pencil. Cut out the whole shape in one piece. Depending on the size of the throat on your scrollsaw, you may have to back out and saw in from different points to complete the cut.

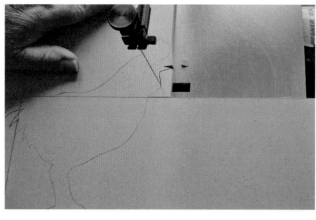

18 Redraw over your pencil outline of the cockerel with a thick black marker pen, then paint the rest of the board with one or two coats of chalkboard paint, allowing it to dry between coats.

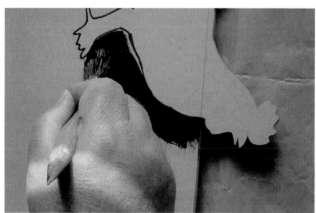

19 When completely dry, turn the board over to position the two strips of wood on the back. Glue one piece 2¾in (70mm) down from the top, and the other 2⅜in (60mm) up from the bottom. When dry, make pilot holes with a bradawl and screw the D-rings into the upper piece.

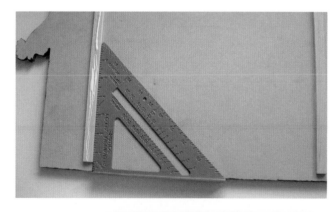

20 Glue the cockerel pieces onto the board, pressing down firmly. It's a good idea to work from head to tail, leaving the feet till last. Wipe off any excess glue with an old artist's paintbrush and allow to dry completely before attaching string or picture wire to the D-rings and hanging the finished board in a handy location, with an easily accessible piece of chalk, to jot down those important reminders.

2:6
Hyacinth macaw key holder

The macaws are a flamboyant group of parrot species from Central and South America; with their bright colours they are amongst the most impressive of all tropical birds. The hyacinth macaw (*Anodorhynchus hyacinthinus*) is one of the most spectacular, both in size and colour. The vibrant ultramarine blue cannot fail to brighten any interior design, and the optional addition of hanging pegs makes it a useful key holder too.

You will need:

- Pine, or other wood of your choice, approx. 36 x 8 x ¾ in (915 x 205 x 19mm)
- ¼ in (6mm) plywood, 24 x 10in (610 x 255mm)
- 3 mini Shaker pegs, 1⅛ x ⁷/₁₆in (28 x 11mm)
- Scrollsaw and no. 7 blade
- Pillar drill with ¼ and ⁵/₁₆in (6 and 8mm) bits
- Disc sander
- Drum sander
- Flexible-shaft tool with rubber-drum sanding kit
- Sanding sleeves, 120 grit
- Wood burner
- Bradawl
- Phillips screwdriver
- 6 copies of the macaw pattern

- Sanding block and sandpaper, 120–320 grit
- Pencil
- Artists' brushes
- Acrylic paints: ultramarine blue, yellow, black
- Acrylic wood stains: light, medium and dark oak
- Slow-dry acrylic medium
- Acrylic varnish: matt, satin and gloss
- Soft, lint-free cloths
- Sanding sealer
- PVA wood glue
- Glue stick
- Tack cloth
- Permanent black marker pens: thick and fine
- Saw-tooth picture hanger and two small screws

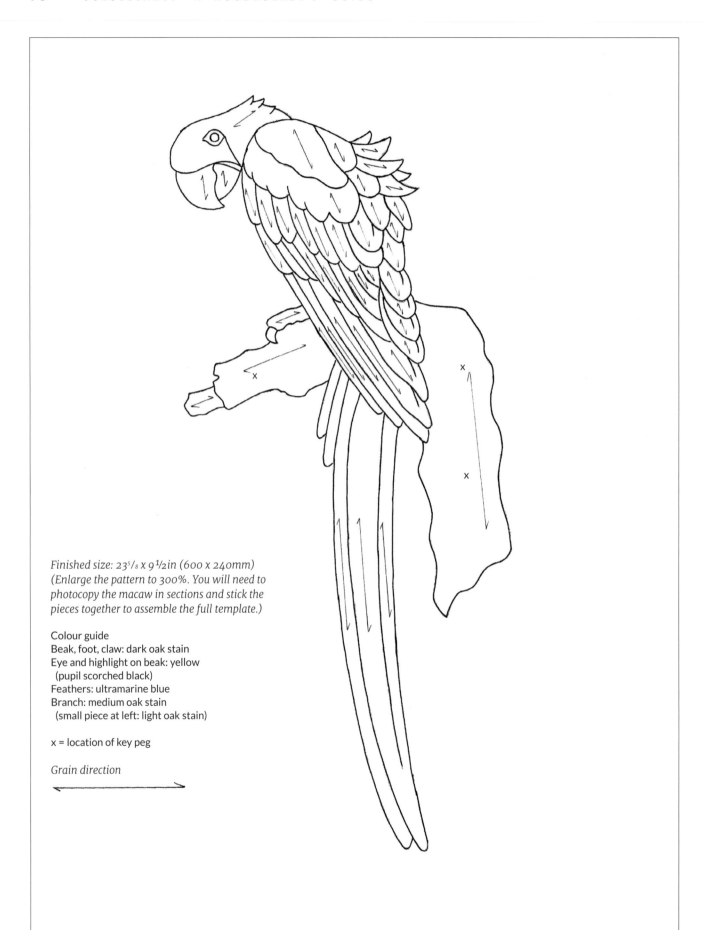

*Finished size: 23⁵/₈ x 9¹/₂in (600 x 240mm)
(Enlarge the pattern to 300%. You will need to
photocopy the macaw in sections and stick the
pieces together to assemble the full template.)*

Colour guide
Beak, foot, claw: dark oak stain
Eye and highlight on beak: yellow
  (pupil scorched black)
Feathers: ultramarine blue
Branch: medium oak stain
  (small piece at left: light oak stain)

x = location of key peg

Grain direction

1 Enlarge the pattern to the size given, taping several sheets of paper together if necessary, and make six copies. Keep one copy for reference: you can write the numbers of the feather pieces on this, to help identify them when all the pieces have been cut up. Note that the pattern falls into eight sections with different grain directions.

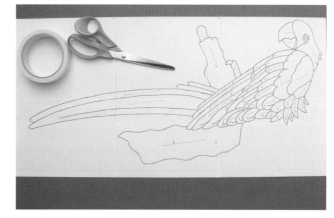

2 Use the remaining five copies of the pattern to cut out these eight sections, leaving a border of approximately 3/8in (10mm) around each. Arrange the patterns on your pine, aligning the grain-direction arrows with the wood grain. If possible, choose a straight-grained part for the long tail feathers and a more curved grain for the top of the wing and head. When happy with the layout of all the pieces, use a glue stick to fix each section firmly to the wood.

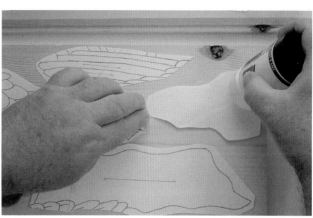

3 It's a good idea to cut the wood into pieces of manageable size before cutting round the detailed outlines. Before you cut out the head piece, drill the hole for the eye, using a 5/16in (8mm) bit in the pillar drill.

4 Fit the scrollsaw with a no. 7 blade. It is important that the wood is flat and the blade straight and taut, as described on page 17. Cut out the main body/wing piece first. De-burr this and every other piece, after cutting, with a piece of 120-grit sandpaper to ensure that all the pieces lie flat when assembled.

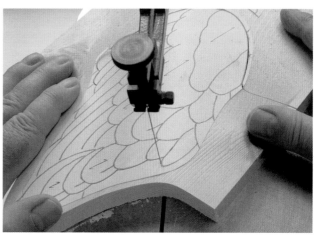

5 Lay the newly cut piece over the next piece to be cut (in this case, the longer wing feathers), and if necessary retrace the cut line onto the new piece. Then check the fit of these two pieces before moving on to the next one.

6 For the small feather pieces on the back of the macaw, cut into the V-shape, back the blade out and move on to the next V, and so on to the end.

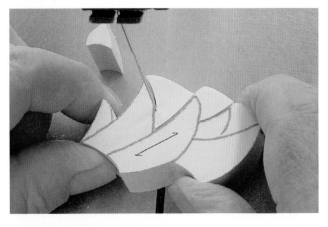

7 Return to cut out the waste.

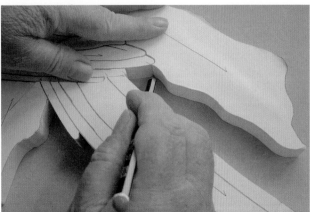

8 When all eight sections have been cut out, put them together to check the fit, and mark with a pencil all the places where one piece meets another.

9 Next, cut up the eight sections into individual pieces, separating the feathers, the foot and claw, the eye, and the upper and lower parts of the beak. Mark the underside of each piece to ensure that you sand the right side. Number the feathers for easy location, and copy these numbers onto the sixth copy of the pattern for reference.

10 Remove as much of the paper pattern as you can by hand; what is left will be easily sanded off at the next stage.

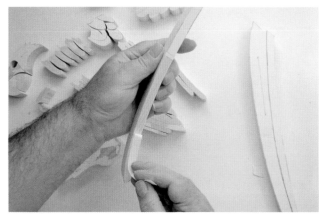

11 Creating different levels of relief will help to give the macaw a three-dimensional appearance. A disc sander fitted with an 80-grit sanding disc is great for rapid waste removal, but be careful: it's easy to take off too much, and you cannot put it back on. Start with the lowest pieces, which will be the branches; lower both of these by ³/₁₆in (5mm).

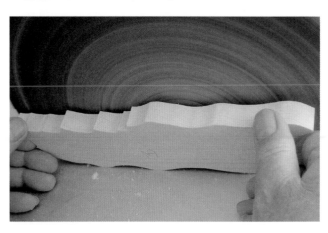

12 Mark the height of the branches on all adjacent pieces: claw, wing and tail feathers.

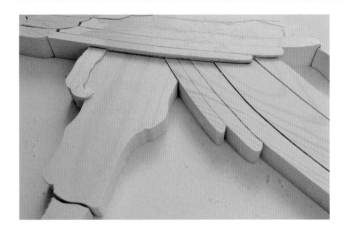

13 Moving on to the claw, lower this by about $5/32$in (4mm). Next come the tail pieces, starting with the one closest to the smaller branch: sand this down by $1/8$in or so (3mm), then lower the rest of the tail pieces by gradually decreasing amounts.

14 The wing and body feathers will need very little sanding; some of the inner pieces will only need the paper pattern removed. Sand the head to approximately $1/16$in (2mm) lower than the body. Already the macaw is taking on a three-dimensional appearance.

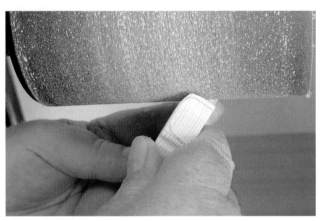

15 The drum and flexible-shaft sanders are very useful tools for rounding over the edges of the pieces, remembering always to sand with the grain to remove any imperfections left by the disc sander. As with the rough sanding, start with the lowest pieces – the branches and tail.

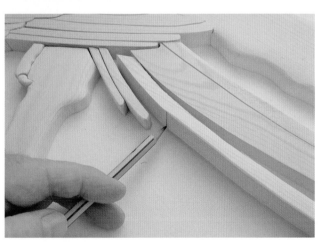

16 Redraw your height marks as you sand each piece, and remember not to sand below these marks. Also be mindful of your pencil lines showing where one piece meets another. Don't be afraid to go back and sand a little more from the previous piece, but take care not to take off too much, especially on the central wing pieces: sand little and often, replacing each piece back in position to check the appearance.

17 The edge feathers can be more strongly rounded; again mark the height and shape of each feather onto the next piece.

18 Thin down the beak and round it over, place it back in position to mark the shape onto the head, then sand the head round and down to the line. The yellow highlight is cut from the beak at this stage; the photo shows this being marked out.

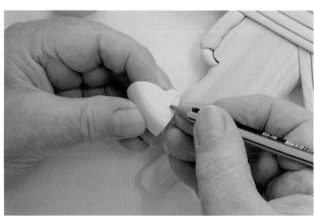

19 Place a length of ⁵⁄₁₆in (8mm) dowel into the pre-drilled hole in the eye, mark the height with a pencil and cut to length on your scrollsaw so that it stands just a little proud of the eyeball. Round over one of the ends with 180-grit sandpaper.

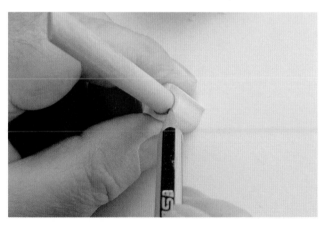

20 Now burn the top of the eye with a wood burner. This will seal the end grain of the dowel better than wood stain, giving the eye a far superior finish. Apply two coats of acrylic gloss varnish with a soft artist's brush, allowing it to dry between coats, to give that extra lustre to the eye.

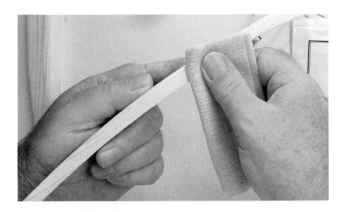

21 Now sand all the pieces by hand. First use the sanding block with 120- to 180-grit paper, to remove any scratches left by drum sanding. Then move on to a 220-grit paper, sanding and rounding over the edges of each piece in turn to a smooth finish. Finally, remove the dust from the pieces with a small, soft brush and a tack cloth.

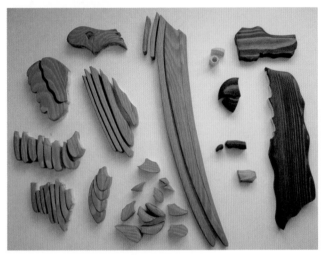

22 Sort the pieces by colour, according to the colour guide on page 78. Mix the colours and acrylic medium together, apply with an artist's brush, then remove any excess with a soft, lint-free cloth to reveal the wood grain beneath. Leave the pieces to dry thoroughly, then carefully rub them down with a very fine 320-grit sandpaper, again wiping away the fine dust with a tack cloth.

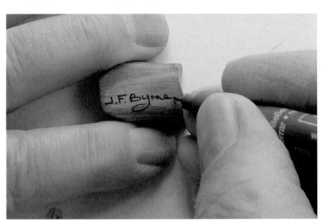

23 To finish, apply one or two coats of acrylic matt varnish to the entire macaw, except the three pieces of the beak, the claw and the yellow part of the eye – use a satin varnish on these pieces to give them a soft sheen. Allow everything to dry overnight. Now is the time to sign your work if you wish, using a fine permanent black marker pen.

24 Assemble all the pieces on the plywood backing sheet. Using a sharp pencil, trace around the whole outline first; then carefully remove one section at a time and mark around the adjoining pieces that are left, until you have a detailed map of all the parts. Cut out the complete outline on the scrollsaw; as the piece is quite long, you may have to reverse the blade out and cut in from a different angle, depending on the throat size of your saw.

25 Apply a coat of sanding sealer to the reverse side; this will help to stop any moisture penetrating through the back, and will also stop the edging colour from running. Go over your inner pencil lines with a thick black marker pen to disguise any slight gaps between the pieces, then apply black acrylic paint around the edges of the backing. When dry, sand the backing with 180-grit paper on a sanding block, and the edges with 320-grit. Wipe down with a tack cloth.

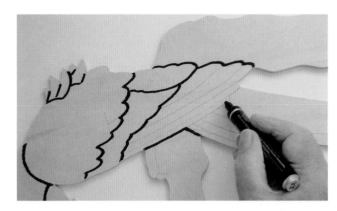

26 Place the backing on a flat surface and assemble all the pieces onto the backing to check the fit. Apply glue to the underside of each piece in turn and glue into place; it should be enough to just push the glued pieces firmly down, without clamping. Wipe off any surplus glue with an old artist's brush or a damp cloth, and allow to dry on the flat surface – the time taken will depend on the glue used.

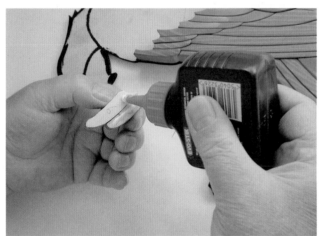

27 Hold up the macaw between your thumb and forefinger until it hangs the way you want, and mark the location for the saw-tooth hanger with a bradawl. Lay the macaw face down on a soft cloth and fit the hanger using the two small screws.

28 Stain and varnish the pegs to match the branches, and allow to dry. Stick small pieces of masking tape on the three peg locations and mark a centre cross on each. Drill the holes just deep enough, using a bit to match the pegs – in our case 1/4in (6mm). Remove the tape and clean out the holes if necessary before applying a small dab of glue to the end of each peg and gluing them into place.

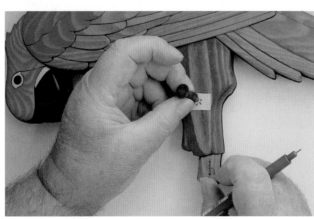

3
Projects for a Child's Room

3:1
Teddy-bear coat rack

3:2
Teddy name plate

3:3
Duck bookends

3:4
Dreaming on the moon

3:1
Teddy-bear coat rack

The teddy motif featured in several of the projects in Part 3 can be used in a variety of ways. Three small teddies are incorporated in this simple coat rack – a fun and practical item to make for any child's room. We have varied the effect by placing a bear-shaped cut-out between the two three-dimensional bears; using the same design in different ways like this is a very effective way of bringing variety to your work without detracting from its overall theme.

You will need:

- Pine, 19¼ x 3¾ x ¾ in (490 x 95 x 19mm)
- Two pieces of ¼in (6mm) sheet wood, 4in (102mm) square: one each of mahogany and birch
- Four 2½in (64mm) Shaker pegs
- Scrollsaw with no.1 and no. 7 blades
- Pillar drill with ⅛ and ⅜in (3 and 9mm) bits
- Pencil
- Photocopied patterns
- Fine permanent black marker pen
- Good-quality PVA wood glue
- Glue stick
- Sanding block and sandpaper, 120–320 grit
- Tack cloth
- Artists' brushes
- Clear acrylic matt varnish
- Bradawl
- Screwdriver
- Mirror plates and screws

Key point

We switched around the parts of the two cut-out teddies so that the colours of one are the negative of the other. This is a traditional technique in marquetry, where it is known as 'counterchange'.

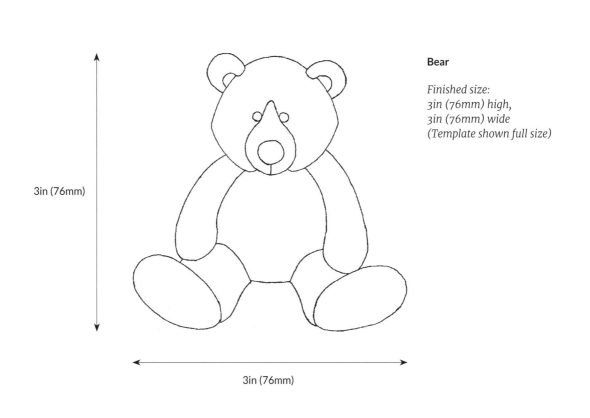

3in (76mm)

3in (76mm)

Bear

Finished size:
3in (76mm) high,
3in (76mm) wide
(Template shown full size)

Rack

Finished size: 19 ¼ x 3 ¾ x ¾ in (490 x 95 x 19mm)

Peg holes: ⅜in (9mm) diameter at 5in (127mm) centres,
1in (25mm) up from bottom edge

(This template needs to be enlarged to 288%. You will
need to photocopy it in sections and stick the pieces
together to assemble the full template.)

1 Begin by preparing the back section of the coat rack; rounding over the edges with a sanding block and 120–180-grit paper is a nice feature, but not essential. Next make two copies of the teddy-bear pattern so they measure 3in (76mm) high. The first will be used to make the central teddy shape. Cut it out, leaving a narrow border all round, then use a ruler to find the centre of the wood, and glue the pattern in place with the glue stick.

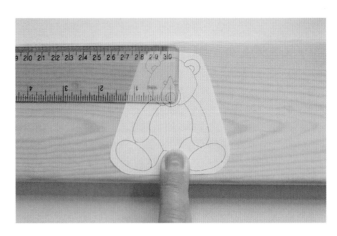

2 Fit a ⅛in (3mm) bit into the pillar drill and make a small hole all the way through the teddy shape, to take the no. 7 scrollsaw blade. Align and tighten the blade as described on page 17. Proceed to cut out the teddy shape, and then remove the remaining pieces of the paper pattern. Use 280-grit sandpaper around the edges to remove the burr from the cut line.

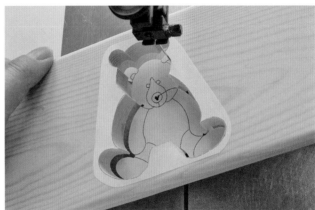

3 Referring to the pattern, measure out and mark the four locations for the pegs. Fit the pillar drill with a bit that matches the diameter of the tenons on the pegs – in our case, ⅜in (9mm). Measure the length of the tenons and mark this depth on the drill bit with a strip of masking tape so as not to drill in too deep; then proceed to drill out the holes.

4 Apply a dab of wood glue to each peg in turn and press firmly into each pre-drilled hole, wiping away any glue that may have seeped out. Then set aside to dry.

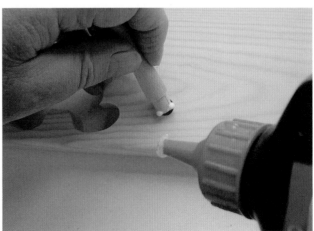

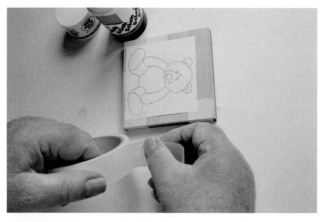

5 Cut out the second paper pattern, then using the glue stick attach it to the birch square, so the grain of the wood runs horizontally across the teddy. Place the mahogany square beneath, with its grain running vertically, and secure both squares together with masking tape.

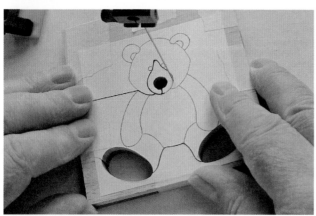

6 Fit the scrollsaw with a no. 1 blade. If your saw does not have a zero-clearance insert fitted (ours doesn't), make a false plywood table top as described on page 19. This stops the very small pieces you are about to cut out from disappearing down the blade space. Cut the inner pieces first, such as the nose and muzzle; this will help the two squares to hold together longer as you progress to cutting the outer pieces.

7 Retain the outer squares to use as a template, to help align the teddy pieces when gluing. Use a pencil to mark the underside of each piece with an L or R to indicate which bear they belong to.

8 Now you can intermix the pieces to make a pair of two-tone teddies. Note the contrasting grain directions in the light and dark woods.

9 Hand-sand the pieces with 320-grit paper to remove the burr and slightly round over the edges. Wipe with a tack cloth to remove the fine dust. Apply a clear acrylic matt varnish to the teddy pieces, the coat rack and pegs, then allow to dry thoroughly.

10 Prepare for gluing by first placing each of the square templates between the end and middle pegs. Have to hand a damp cloth and an old artist's brush, to wipe away any glue that oozes out, before it dries. Apply a small dab of glue to the underside of each piece in turn. When finished, carefully remove the template and check that the teddy pieces are positioned correctly. Set aside to allow the glue to dry completely.

11 Turn the coat rack over, use a ruler and pencil to find and mark the centre point at each end, then position each mirror plate centrally over your pencil marks.

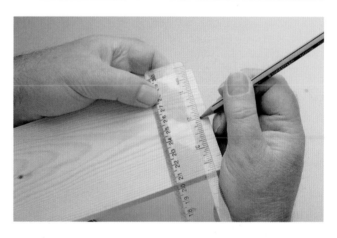

12 Use a bradawl to make pilot holes for the screws, then finally screw the mirror plates on. Now all that is left to do is to screw the coat rack to the wall, and your children will have a secure and fun place to hang their coats and jumpers.

3:2
Teddy name plate

This cuddly teddy name plate-cum-chalkboard will be great for young and older children alike. The young can learn to write their own name, while older children will probably write Keep out! As an alternative, if you want the name or message on the board to be permanent, you could make it with cut-out letters as described on page 171.

You will need:
- ¼in (6mm) birch plywood, 12 x 11in (305 x 280mm)
- Pine, 14 x 6½ x ¾in (356 x 165 x 19mm)
- Small offcut of ⁵/₃₂in (4mm) plywood (to fit behind the nose and muzzle)
- Four 2½in (64mm) Shaker pegs
- Scrollsaw with no. 5 and no. 7 blades
- Disc sander
- Drum and flexible-shaft sanders with 120-grit sanding sleeves
- Screwdriver
- Pencil
- Photocopied patterns
- Fine permanent black marker pen
- PVA wood glue
- Glue stick
- Sanding block and sandpaper, 180–320 grit
- Tack cloth
- Wood burner
- Artists' brushes and 1in (25mm) household paintbrush
- Matt black (chalkboard) paint
- Acrylic wood stains: light oak and medium oak
- Acrylic matt black paint
- Acrylic matt varnish
- Clear wax polish
- D-ring and screw or screws
- Bradawl

Finished size: 7¼in (185mm) high, 7¼in (185mm) wide
(This template needs to be enlarged to 111%)

Grain direction

Colour guide
Centre of nose: medium oak stain
Muzzle, outer parts of ears: light oak stain, diluted with acrylic medium
All other parts: light oak stain

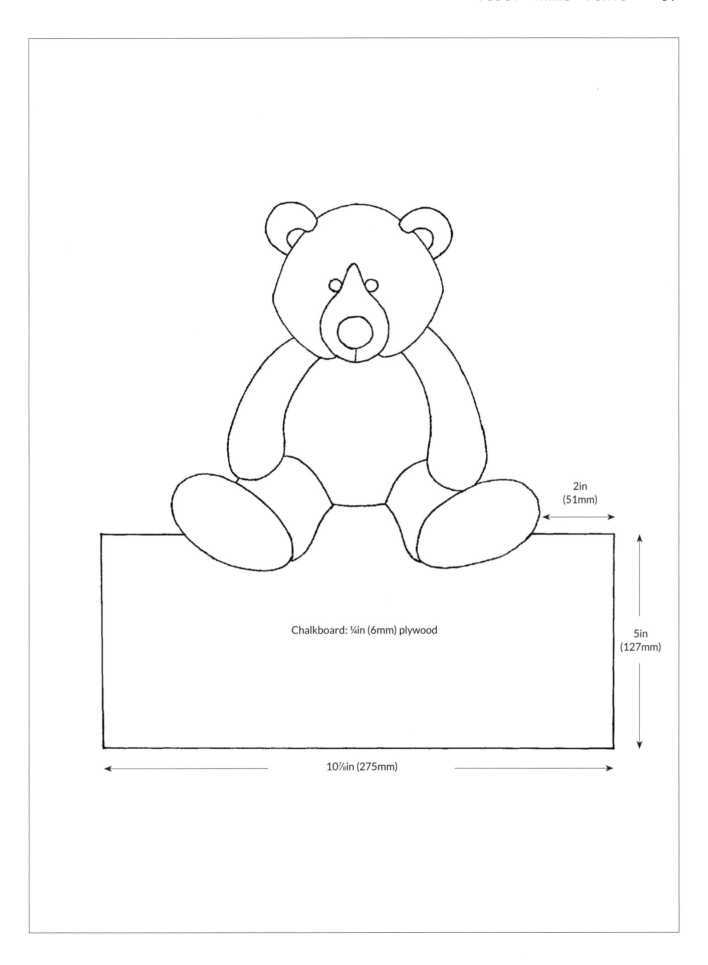

2in
(51mm)

Chalkboard: ¼in (6mm) plywood

5in
(127mm)

10⅞in (275mm)

1 To begin, make three copies of the teddy bear pattern, 7¼ in (185mm) square. Cut the three copies into seven sections as shown, and lay the pattern on the wood so that the directional arrows match the wood grain. Use the glue stick to secure the pattern to the wood.

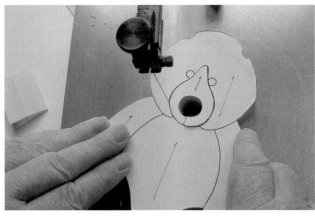

2 Cut out the head, body and arm piece first, then the ears; check that they both fit onto the head properly before moving on to cut out legs and feet. Then separate the head, body and arms.

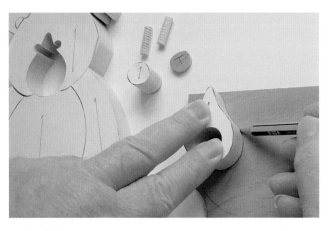

3 To give more relief to the muzzle and nose pieces, place these on the offcut of thin plywood and trace around each piece with a pencil.

4 Cut out about ¹⁄₁₆in (2mm) inside the line. The plywood packing will then easily fit in place behind the other pieces.

5 Sanding down the parts of the teddy to different height levels and rounding over the outer edges will help give the figure a three-dimensional appearance. Use the disc sander first to create the different levels. Sand the tummy down by $5/32$in (4mm), presenting the piece to the sander with a rocking motion from side to side, so the middle stays a little higher to give the teddy a nice rounded tummy.

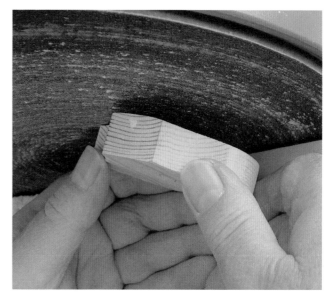

6 Mark the height of this piece onto each leg and sand to the line, but not below. Then mark the height of the legs onto the feet; these will hardly need any sanding down at all, perhaps $1/32$ or $1/16$in (1 or 2mm) above the line. Next mark the height of the body and legs onto each arm, then lower and round over the outer edges of the arms, but staying approximately $1/16$in (2mm) above your line. The head piece needs only the outer edges rounded over slightly, and the inner ear pieces sanded level with the head.

7 All the rest of the sanding can be done with the drum and flexible-shaft sanders, remembering always to sand with the grain, to remove any scratches left by the disc sander. It's just a matter of rounding over all the outer edges, being mindful not to sand below your pencil lines. Once again start with the tummy, and try to keep the middle nice and plump-looking. Shape each piece, re-marking your pencil lines on the adjoining pieces as you go. The photo shows half the bear sanded in this way.

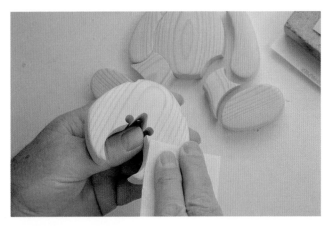

8 When you are happy with the shape of the teddy bear, it's time to hand-sand the pieces smooth. Start with 120-grit sandpaper and the sanding block, then use a piece of 180-grit paper folded in half, and finish by using the pressure of your thumb to follow the shape of the pieces. Take your time: the finishing is just as important as the cutting. Use a soft brush and then a tack cloth to remove the dust from the pieces.

9 Assemble the teddy pieces together onto the large piece of plywood, 5in (127mm) up from the bottom edge; centre the teddy so there is 2in (51mm) of plywood either side of the feet. Then, using a sharp pencil, draw around the outline of the teddy, down to the top of the chalkboard area.

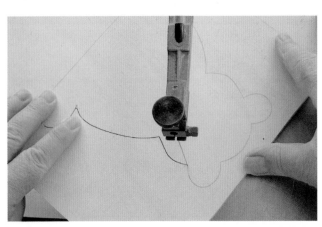

10 Change the scrollsaw blade to a no. 5. Start the cut along the 2in (51mm) straight line, then go up and over the shape of the teddy, finishing the cut on the other straight line going out. Apply a sanding sealer to the back of the plywood and allow to dry, then lightly nib down with 280-grit paper, wiping with a tack cloth to remove the fine dust.

11 Paint the chalkboard area with a special matt chalkboard paint; you may need to apply two coats. When dry, use an artist's brush to apply an acrylic matt black paint all around the edges, to give a more finished look.

12 We stained most of the figure with an acrylic light oak wood stain, making it lighter for the muzzle and ear pieces by adding acrylic medium. The nose is coloured a shade darker with a medium oak wood stain. The tops of the eyes were burnt with a wood burner; you could use a darker wood stain or a black or dark brown felt pen. Allow to dry, then very lightly rub down with 320-grit sandpaper, again wiping down with a tack cloth.

13 Apply an acrylic matt varnish, with contrasting gloss varnish on the nose and eyes. When dry, once again lightly rub down and wipe over with the tack cloth. If you wish, now is a good time to sign one of the pieces, using a fine permanent black marker. Finally, add a coat of wax polish to the front and edges – not the back – of all pieces except the eyes, and buff to a nice sheen.

14 Before assembling the teddy, have a damp cloth and an old artist's brush to hand, to wipe away any glue that may ooze out. Apply glue to the back of the head and press firmly into place, then glue on the ears. Attach the plywood thickening piece for the muzzle, followed by the muzzle itself, and glue the nose pieces in the same way. Add all the other pieces in turn, finishing with the feet, and wipe away any excess glue before it dries.

15 When everything is dry, attach a D-ring to the back. Find the right place for it by holding the teddy between your thumb and finger until it hangs level. Laying the piece face down on a soft cloth, use a bradawl to make the pilot hole or holes, and screw the D-ring in position with a Phillips screwdriver. All this teddy needs now is a door to hang on and a piece of chalk!

3:3
Duck bookends

There are three good reasons to make these fun duck bookends: your children will love them, and they will keep their books in order and the shelf or bookcase tidy. It's never too soon to introduce them to good habits!

You will need:

- Parana pine for the bookends, 24 x 3½ x ¾in (610 x 89 x 19mm)
- Pine for the ducks, 24 x 4 x ¾in (610 x 102 x 19mm)
- ¼in (6mm) birch plywood, 10in (254mm) square
- Two short lengths of hardwood dowel, $^{11}/_{16}$in (9mm) and $^5/_{32}$in (4mm) diameter
- Small offcut of $^5/_{32}$in (4mm) plywood (to fit behind the wings and beaks)
- Scrollsaw and no. 7 blade
- Disc sander
- Drum and flexible-shaft sanders with 120-grit sanding sleeves
- Bradawl
- Pillar drill with ⅛, $^5/_{32}$ and ⅜in (3, 4 and 9mm) bits
- Four 1¼in no. 8 (32 x 4mm) screws
- Phillips screwdriver
- Spring clamp
- Wood burner

- Pencil
- Try square or engineer's square
- Ruler
- Small set square
- Photocopied patterns
- PVA wood glue
- Glue stick
- Sanding block and sandpaper, 180–320 grit
- Tack cloth
- Artists' brushes
- Acrylic paint: yellow, white and matt black
- Acrylic wood stain: cedar
- Acrylic medium
- Acrylic matt varnish
- Clear wax polish
- Soft cloth or brush for buffing

Key point

You could use other figures instead of the ducks, but remember that characters in books or cartoons are protected by copyright – you would be breaking the law if you copied a well-known character and then offered your work for sale.

Finished size: 7½ x 3in (192 x 77mm)
(Pattern shown full size)

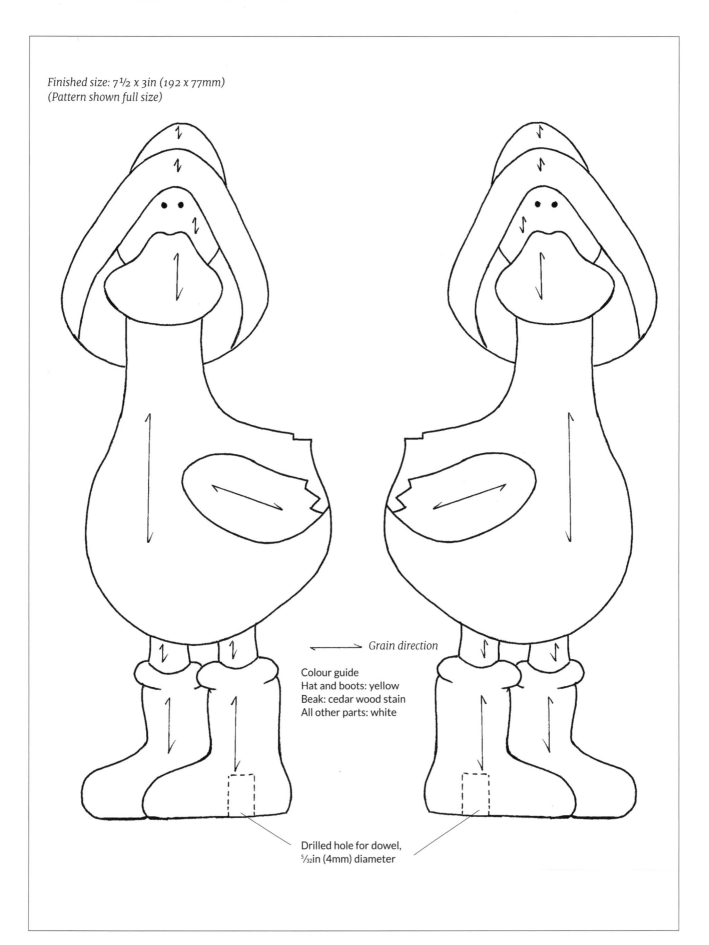

Grain direction

Colour guide
Hat and boots: yellow
Beak: cedar wood stain
All other parts: white

Drilled hole for dowel,
5/32in (4mm) diameter

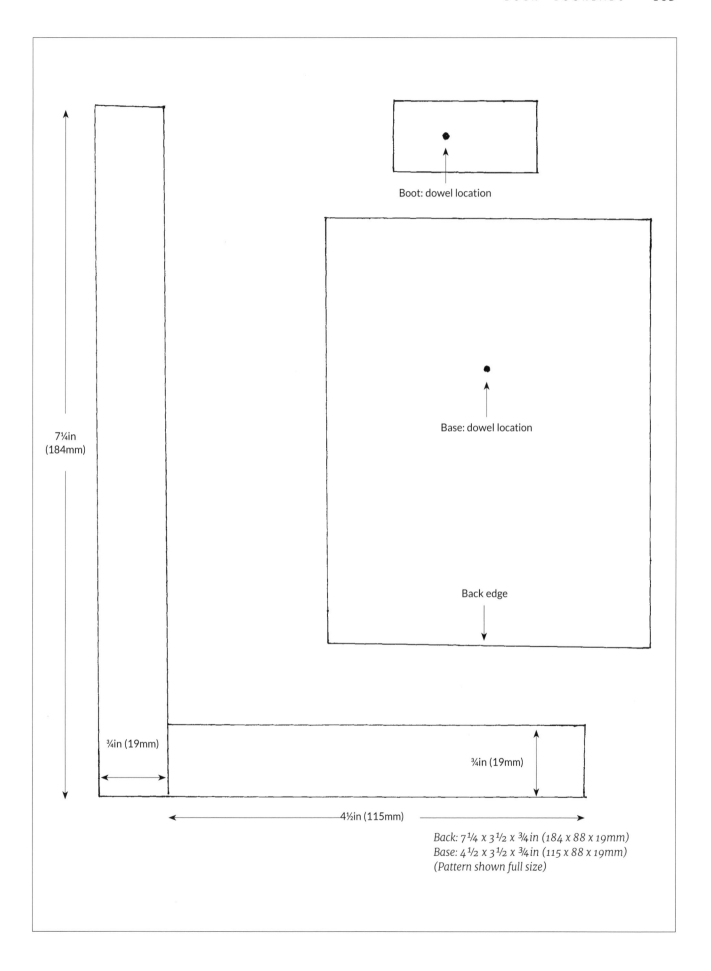

7¼in
(184mm)

Boot: dowel location

Base: dowel location

Back edge

¾in (19mm)

¾in (19mm)

4½in (115mm)

Back: 7¼ x 3½ x ¾in (184 x 88 x 19mm)
Base: 4½ x 3½ x ¾in (115 x 88 x 19mm)
(Pattern shown full size)

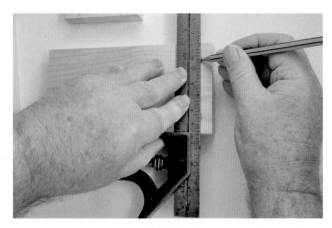

1 Begin by marking out the measurements for the backs and bases on your Parana pine, or whatever wood you have chosen. The dimensions are given in the drawing. Set up the scrollsaw with a no. 7 blade, aligned and tightened as described on page 17. Cut out the four pieces and smooth the edges with 180-grit sandpaper on a sanding block.

2 The bases and backs will be screwed together. Fit a $1/8$in (3mm) bit in the pillar drill, then lay the two back uprights face down and mark the hole positions, measuring up $3/8$in (10mm) from the bottom and $3/4$in (19mm) in from either side. Align each mark in turn under the pillar drill and clamp to secure, then drill each hole all the way through.

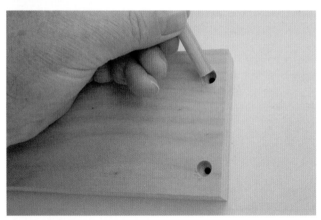

3 Change to a larger $3/8$in (9mm) bit, and countersink each hole to a depth of about $1/4$in (6mm); this will allow the screw heads to be covered by short lengths of dowel. Working on a flat surface, match each base to its upright back piece. Apply glue to the end of the base, align the back upright in position, then drive in the screws to secure. If any glue oozes out, wipe away with a damp cloth.

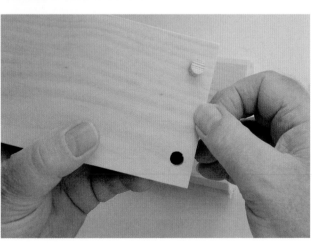

4 Cut four lengths of $3/8$in (9mm) dowel just a fraction longer than the depth of the countersinking. Place a small dab of glue into each hole, align the dowel plugs with the grain of the wood, then cover each dowel in turn with a small piece of plywood to protect it as you hammer it home. Allow the glue to cure completely, then sand the dowels flush with the back, using 180-grit paper on a sanding block. Finish the bookends with acrylic matt varnish.

5 Make two copies of the duck pattern facing right, and two facing left. The wing has a different grain direction from the rest of the duck, so it will need to be cut out separately. Attach the patterns to the wood using a glue stick. In the photo, Fred has just made a reference mark across the joint between body and legs, so they can be repositioned accurately after cutting out. Make similar marks where the hat meets the neck on each side.

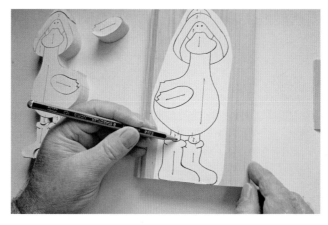

6 Cut out the wing pieces first, and check them against the duck body; if they don't quite match, redraw around the wing with a sharp pencil and then follow this new cut line. Continue sawing until all the pieces of the two ducks have been cut out. For the tips of the wing feathers, use one of the techniques described on pages 20–1. Before removing the pattern, mark each piece on the back to show which duck it belongs to.

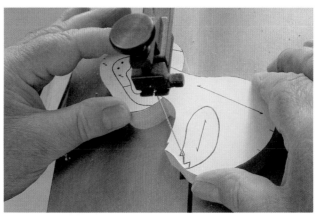

7 From a scrap of thin plywood, cut packing pieces to fit underneath the wing and beak so that they will stand proud of the rest of the surface. Trace round the wing and beak pieces, and cut the plywood slightly undersize.

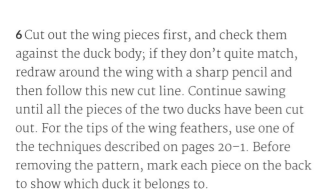

8 Dowels are used to give the duck added strength, and for easier location when gluing it to the bookend. Fit the pillar drill with a ⁵⁄₃₂in (4mm) bit, then glue the small locating pattern to the underside of the boot, which is held with a spring clamp. Check, using a small set square, that the boot is square to the drill bit, before drilling down ½in (13mm).

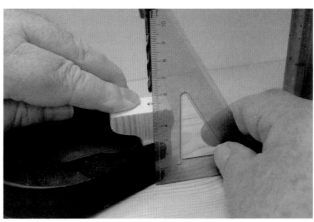

9 Place the larger locating pattern onto the base of the bookend, making sure the back edge of the pattern is against the upright of the bookend, then push a bradawl through the pattern and into the wood. Clamp the bookend under the pillar drill and bore the hole as before.

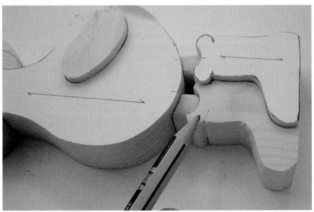

10 Use the disc sander to lower the legs by ⁵/₃₂in (4mm) and the top of the hat by ³/₁₆in (5mm). The rest of the shaping can be done with the drum and flexible-shaft sanders. Round over the sides of the legs, then mark the height of each leg onto the body and boots. Shape the rear boot to just above your pencil line, then mark the height of this boot onto the front boot and shape this in the same way; the nearer boot stands a little bit proud of the other.

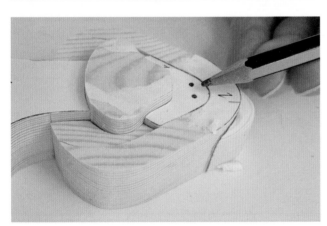

11 Shape the hat so the front part stays high and the sides of the brim taper down to the bottom. Make the inner hat pieces level with the bottom edge of the brim, then make their inner edges slope towards the head, to give the illusion that the brim passes behind the neck. Take the head down so it is just a little lower than the top of the hat, but higher than the inner hat pieces.

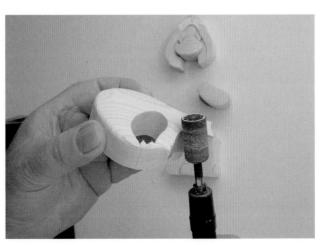

12 Mark the height of the hat on both sides of the neck, then round and shape the whole body. Use the flexible-shaft tool, fitted with a small-diameter sanding sleeve, to sand those small inner curves, but be mindful not to sand lower than your height marks.

13 Lastly, mark a pencil line around the raised beak and wing pieces, taper back the top part of the beak while leaving the lower part high, and shape the wing to ¹⁄₁₆in (2mm) above the body. Hand-sand all the pieces to a smooth finish, first with 120 and then moving on to 180-grit paper. Wipe down with a tack cloth to remove the fine dust.

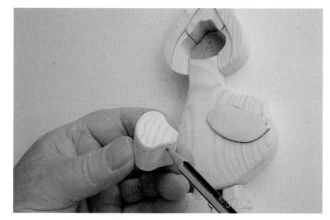

14 Assemble the two ducks on the ¼in (6mm) plywood, and draw around each duck with a sharp pencil. Use the scrollsaw to cut out the two plywood backing pieces. If you wish to remove the small piece between the legs, first drill a small hole to feed the blade through, as shown; otherwise, just paint this small piece black. Lightly sand the edges, remove the fine dust with a tack cloth, and paint the edges matt black.

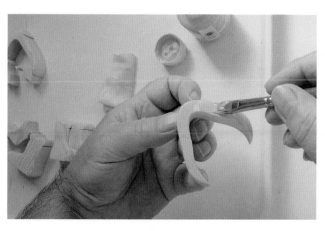

15 Colour the ducks in the usual way, mixing each colour with medium for greater transparency, and wipe off the excess. Very lightly rub down with 320-grit sandpaper, then wipe over again with a tack cloth. Referring to the pattern, use a pencil to mark the dots for the eyes, then carefully burn these in using a small circular bit fitted into the wood burner. Alternatively, paint the eyes black. Apply acrylic matt varnish to all pieces, polish and buff.

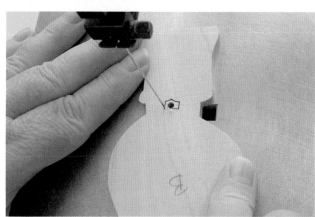

16 Glue each piece in turn onto the plywood backing, working down from the hat to the boots. When dry, put a drop of glue in the small drilled hole in the base, then insert a 1in (25mm) length of ⁵⁄₃₂in (4mm) dowel. Add more glue to the dowel and to the underside of the boots, then align the dowel with the hole in the boot and push the duck firmly into place. Allow everything to dry completely before handling.

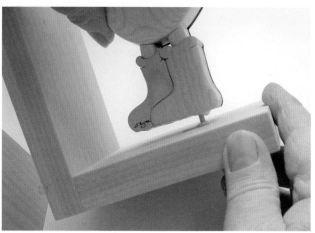

3:4
Dreaming on the moon

Whatever the time of year, this little wall hanging showing a teddy sleeping on the moon would make a lovely gift for a little one. It is quite a versatile pattern: you could convert it into a hanging mobile by making a mirror-image pair, using thinner wood, and gluing them back to back, or simply by cutting the outline from one piece of wood and painting the figure in your own choice of colours. All in all, a thoroughly fun project to do.

You will need:

· Pine, 25 x 6¾ x ¾ in (630 x 170 x 19mm)
· ¼ in (6mm) plywood, 13 x 12½ in (330 x 320mm)
· Scrollsaw and no. 7 blade
· Disc sander
· Drum and flexible-shaft sanders with rubber-drum sanding kit
· Bradawl
· Screwdriver
· Sanding block and sandpaper, 120–320 grit
· Tracing paper
· Carbon paper
· Pencil
· Artists' brushes
· Acrylic paints: white, black, yellow and burnt sienna
· Slow-dry acrylic medium
· Acrylic matt or satin varnish
· Clear wax polish
· Soft cloths or brush for buffing
· Sanding sealer
· PVA wood glue
· Tack cloth
· Permanent black marker pens: thick and fine
· D-ring and small screw

Finished size: 11 ¾ x 11 ½in (300 x 290mm)
(Enlarge pattern to 188%)

Colour guide
Moon: white
Main part of teddy: yellow mixed with a little
  burnt sienna
Inner ear and mouth pieces: same colour,
  lightened with white
Nose: black

Grain direction

1 This time we have shown the more traditional method of transferring the pattern to the wood, using carbon paper, but feel free to use the glue stick instead if you prefer. Enlarge the pattern to approximately the dimensions given, and transfer the pattern onto the tracing paper. Trace each piece individually onto the pine using the carbon paper, lining up the arrows on the pattern with the wood grain as you trace each piece.

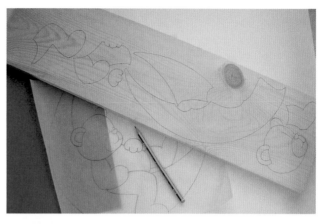

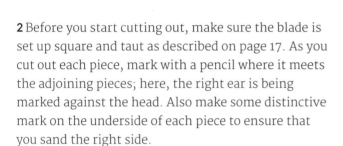

2 Before you start cutting out, make sure the blade is set up square and taut as described on page 17. As you cut out each piece, mark with a pencil where it meets the adjoining pieces; here, the right ear is being marked against the head. Also make some distinctive mark on the underside of each piece to ensure that you sand the right side.

3 Using a disc sander fitted with 120-grit sandpaper, thin down the lower part of the moon by $^5/_{32}$in (4mm), and a little more towards the outer edge.

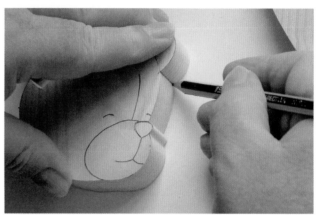

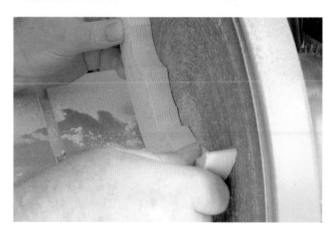

4 Transfer this height measurement to the top half of the moon; this will ensure the height of the moon runs consistent throughout, when you come to sand the top half, so that it looks as though it is all one piece.

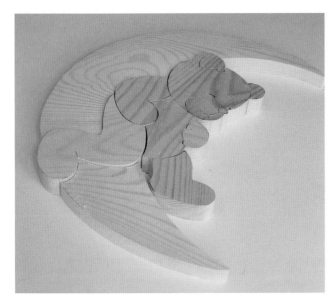

5 Sand down the bear's left ear by ¼in (6mm), and mark this height onto the side of the head. Lower the left leg by ³/₁₆in (5mm), so it sits just below the moon; mark this height onto the tummy and moon. Sand down the tummy by ⅛in (3mm), not going lower than the leg mark, then mark the height of the tummy onto all adjoining pieces.

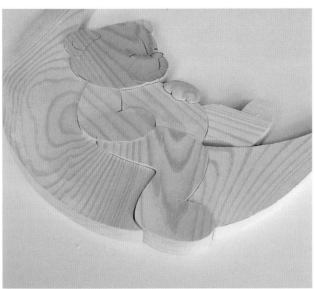

6 Carefully sand down the top of the right leg, by about ¹/₃₂ or ¹/₁₆in (1 or 2mm); try to leave the foot part higher. Lower the left hand, remembering not to sand lower than the tummy height mark. Very lightly sand down the top of the right arm where it meets the head, taking care not to sand below any of your height marks. By creating these different levels, the sleeping teddy is already taking on a three-dimensional appearance.

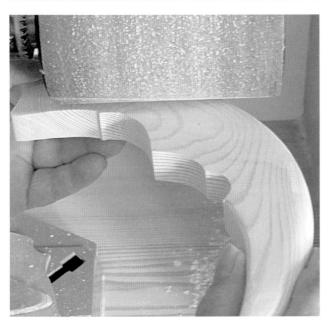

7 The drum sander is now used to round off all the pieces, starting with the outer edges of the moon and always working with the grain. Pay attention to your height marks, and to the areas where one piece meets another. Offer the moon pieces against the teddy, and keep sanding down and round until you are satisfied.

8 Shape and round all the edges of the teddy's left foot, apart from where it joins onto the tummy and lower moon section. A flexible-shaft tool with a small-diameter drum sander is the best tool for tight corners. Round the tummy in the same way, but not the inside edge where it meets the arm and leg; also be careful not to sand below your height marks. The left hand and leg need very little sanding, only to round the edges slightly.

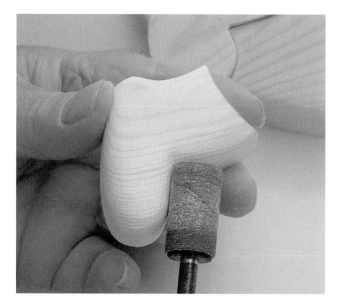

9 Sand the head round towards the left ear mark and down towards the muzzle, rounding over the edges. Sand the inner piece of the right ear a little lower than the head, then round off the outer ear piece to the height marks. Holding the two pieces of the mouth area together, round the outside edges. Round off the nose. Hand-sand all the pieces with 180-grit paper and remove the dust with a tack cloth.

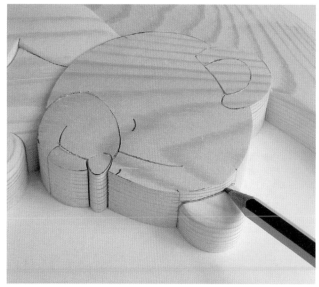

10 Place all the pieces together on your plywood backing sheet and then draw around the outline with a pencil.

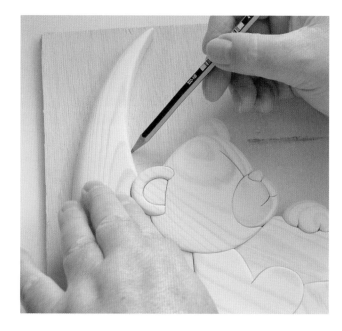

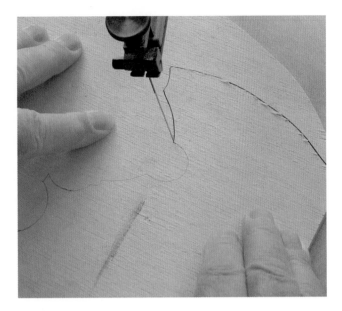

11 Using the scrollsaw, carefully cut out the plywood backing following the outline you have made. Then very lightly sand around the edges, using 320-grit paper. We like to seal the back with a sanding sealer. We also use matt black paint or a thick black permanent marker pen around the edges of the backing, to give the piece a more finished appearance.

12 Sort the pieces into groups for colouring. As usual, add a little slow-dry medium to the paint to give a longer 'open time', and wipe off excess after a few moments so the wood grain can show through. Allow to dry overnight before rubbing down carefully with 320-grit sandpaper and wiping with a tack cloth to remove any fine dust.

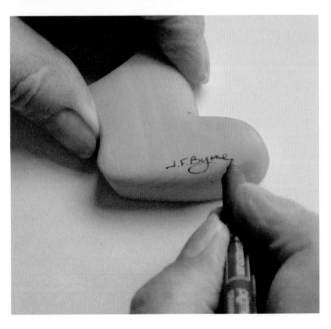

13 Finish all the pieces with an acrylic matt or satin varnish, wiping off any surplus with a clean, soft cloth. When fully dry, sand with 320-grit and wipe with a tack cloth. If you wish, now is the time to sign your work, using a fine waterproof marker pen.

14 Using the pattern and the carbon paper, pencil in the small lines for the closed eyes, then draw these in using the same marker pen. Apply a coat of clear polish to all the pieces, and buff up to a nice shine with a soft cloth or brush.

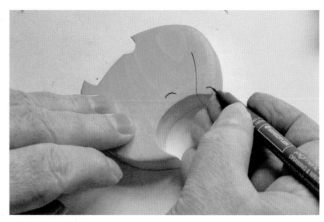

15 Assemble all the pieces onto the plywood backing. Removing one piece at a time, draw around the outlines of every piece with a sharp pencil. Then, using a thick black marker pen, draw over all your pencil lines. This will help to disguise any slight gaps between the pieces.

16 Glue all the pieces onto the backing with good-quality PVA, pressing down each piece firmly as you go. Start with the upper section of the moon, then the left leg, next the lower moon piece and then the rest of the teddy. When all is completely dry, suspend the nearly finished piece between your finger and thumb, as shown, until it hangs at the angle you require. Mark this location on the back with a pencil.

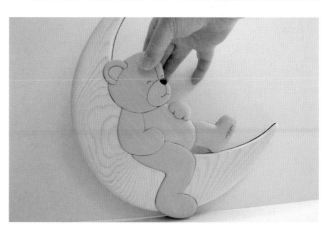

17 Laying the piece face down on a soft cloth, make a pilot hole with the bradawl before screwing the D-ring into place.

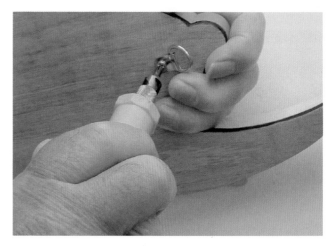

4

Bathroom Projects

4:1
Facecloth holder

This peg rail for holding facecloths can be made to co-ordinate with the towel rail on pages 127–31. Use your own choice of colours to suit your decor, and then choose from the selection of different motifs we have provided.

You will need:

- Tongue-and-groove pine, 24 x 4½ x¾ in (610 x 114 x 19mm)
- Whitewood moulding, 37 x 1 x ½ in (940 x 25 x 13mm)
- Four 1½ in (38mm) Shaker pegs
- Birchwood sheet, 12 x 4 x ⅛in (305 x 102 x 3mm)
- Scrollsaw with no. 1 and no. 7 blades
- Pillar drill and ¼ in (6mm) drill bit
- Try square
- Ruler
- Pencil
- Photocopied patterns
- PVA wood glue, weatherproof (water-resistant)
- Two G-clamps (C-clamps)
- Glue stick

- Sanding block and 180–320-grit sandpaper
- Tack cloth
- Artists' brushes
- Wood primer, undercoat and topcoat of your choice for the peg rail (we used a white water-based eggshell paint)
- Acrylic paint for the motifs: green, blue, yellow, orange and white
- Acrylic medium
- Pair of 1¼ in (32mm) mirror plates with screws
- Phillips screwdriver
- Bradawl
- ¾ in (19mm) panel pins
- Pin hammer
- Nail set
- Wood filler, neutral
- Palette knife or flexible filler knife

Key point

Don't forget to use water-resistant adhesives and finishes for all your bathroom projects – they will be exposed to humid conditions every day. Use weatherproof PVA rather than the ordinary kind. Acrylic paints and stains are ideal.

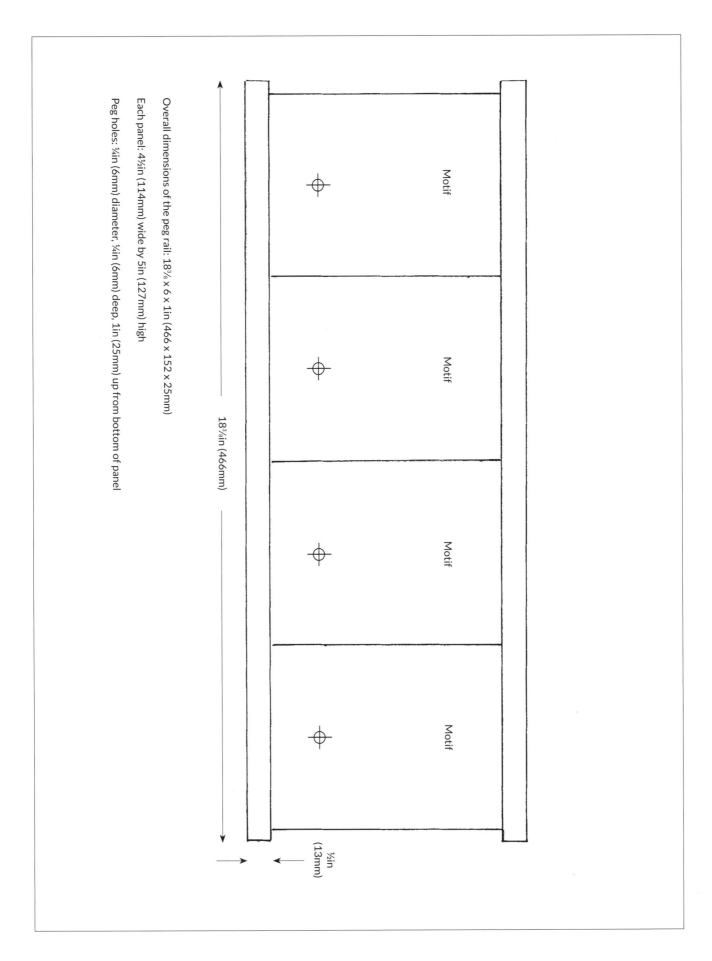

Overall dimensions of the peg rail: 18³/₈ x 6 x 1in (466 x 152 x 25mm)

Each panel: 4½in (114mm) wide by 5in (127mm) high

Peg holes: ¼in (6mm) diameter, ¼in (6mm) deep, 1in (25mm) up from bottom of panel

18³/₈in (466mm)

½in (13mm)

Motif

Motif

Motif

Motif

Enlarge these patterns as required
(see pages 124 and 131).

1 Using a no. 7 blade, cut the tongue-and-groove board into 5in (127mm) lengths. Measure 1in (25mm) up from the bottom edge of each piece, then measure the centre of the width of the board (ignoring the tongue), and mark a cross at this point. Drill a ¼in (6mm) hole ¼in (6mm) deep into each of the four pieces. Cut off the unwanted tongue from one end piece and glue it into the groove at the opposite end. Make good with filler, and sand when dry.

2 Cut the wood moulding into two lengths of 18³⁄8in (466mm) and lay out all the pieces together to check the fit. A try square and ruler will help to ensure that everything is straight and square. Sand all the pieces smooth with 180-grit paper on a sanding block, then wipe down with a tack cloth to remove the fine dust.

3 Assemble the four panels, then glue and tack on the top and bottom mouldings, using a nail set to punch the pins below the surface (the holes can later be stopped with wood filler). Secure with G-clamps (C-clamps) while the glue cures. Glue in the four pegs. If you are going to paint the peg rail, use a wood primer first, then undercoat and topcoat. Allow each coat to dry thoroughly, and rub down lightly with 280-grit sandpaper before applying the next.

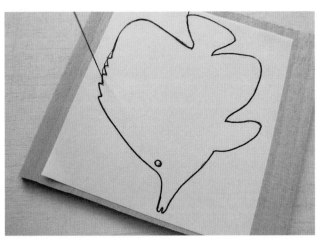

4 Sand your sheet of birch smooth. Choose which of the five motifs you wish to use, and photocopy them to a suitable size, say 2 or 3in (50 or 75mm) high. Cut these out and attach them to the birch with the glue stick. Set the scrollsaw up with a no. 1 blade; if you don't have a zero-clearance insert, make one as described on page 19. Set a fairly slow speed and carefully cut out the small motifs.

5 Before colouring the motifs, remove the paper patterns, lightly sand around the edges with 320-grit paper and remove the dust with a tack cloth. You might also like to burn in the eyes of the fish and seahorse with a wood burner.

6 Mix your chosen colours with a little acrylic medium to help them flow. We painted the seahorse green, the starfish orange, the fish blue and the shell yellow, adding a little white to each colour to give a pastel effect. Wipe off excess paint with a soft cloth and allow to dry. Apply an acrylic matt varnish to the four motifs, and again leave to dry.

7 Lay the peg rail on a flat surface and arrange the motifs in a pleasing order. Apply small dabs of glue to the back of each motif and spread out evenly with an old acrylic brush, then position the motifs and press firmly down onto the peg rail. Allow to dry.

8 Attach the mirror plates to the back of the rail on either side, using two screws for each. Two more screws will be needed to attach the rail to the bathroom wall.

4:2
Towel rail

You can make this towel rail to co-ordinate with the previous project, ensuring all your bathroom fittings match. You could substitute your own choice of colours and motifs if you want it to be really individual.

You will need:

- Tongue-and-groove pine, 48 x 4½ x ¾ in (1220 x 114 x 19mm)
- Two pieces of pine, each 5 x 5 x ¾ in (127 x 127 x 19mm)
- Whitewood moulding, 60 x 1 x ½ in (1525 x 25 x 13mm)
- Birchwood sheet, 12 x 4 x ⅛ in (305 x 102 x 3mm)
- 1in (25mm) hardwood dowel, 24in (610mm) long
- Scrollsaw with no. 1 and no. 7 blades
- Try square
- Ruler
- Pencil
- Photocopied patterns
- PVA wood glue
- Glue stick

- Hammer
- Panel pins, 1½ and ¾ in (38 and 19mm)
- Nail set
- Neutral wood filler
- Sanding block and sandpaper, 180–320 grit
- Artists' brushes
- Tack cloth
- Wood primer, undercoat and topcoat of your choice (we used a white water-based eggshell paint)
- Acrylic paint: green, blue, orange and white
- Acrylic medium
- Two end sockets with fixings
- Two 1½ in (38mm) mirror plates with fixings
- Phillips screwdriver
- Bradawl

Key point

Because the towel rail is made up from sections of tongue-and-groove joined side by side, you can alter the length if necessary by using more or fewer pieces, to suit the space available in your own bathroom.

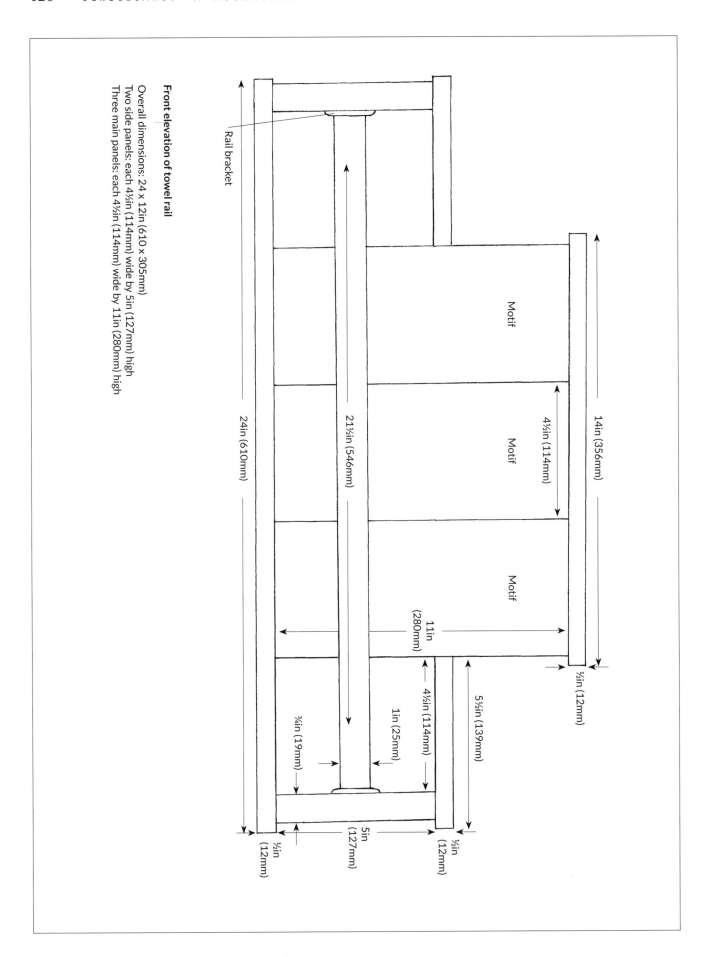

Front elevation of towel rail

Overall dimensions: 24 x 12in (610 x 305mm)
Two side panels: each 4½in (114mm) wide by 5in (127mm) high
Three main panels: each 4½in (114mm) wide by 11in (280mm) high

Rail bracket

14in (356mm)

Motif

Motif

Motif

4½in (114mm)

24in (610mm)

21½in (546mm)

11in (280mm)

½in (12mm)

5½in (139mm)

4½in (114mm)

1in (25mm)

¾in (19mm)

½in (12mm)

5in (127mm)

½in (12mm)

½in (12mm)

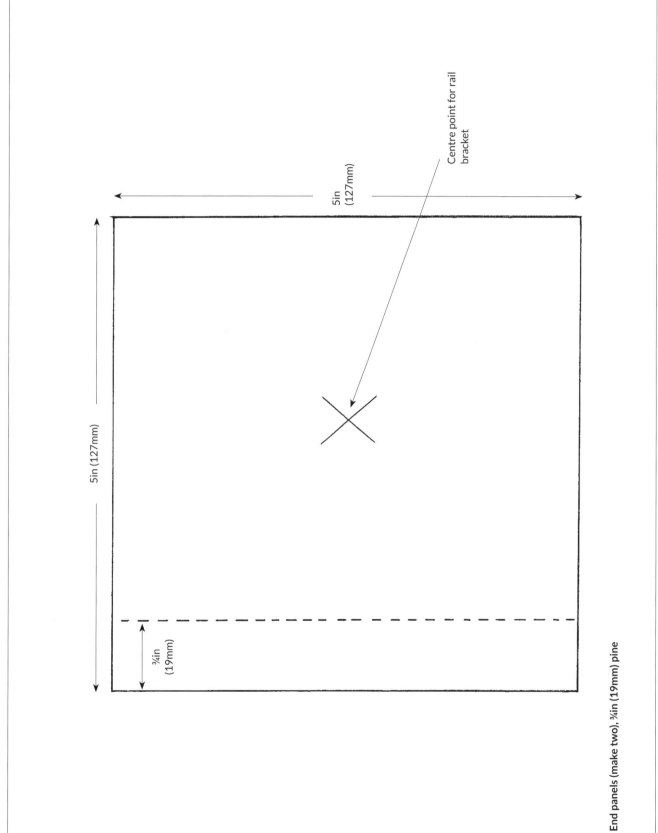

Centre point for rail bracket

5in (127mm)

5in (127mm)

¾in (19mm)

End panels (make two), ¾in (19mm) pine

1 Cut the tongue-and-groove board into five pieces: three main panels 11in (280mm) long, and two side panels 5in (127mm) long. Remove the unwanted tongue-and-groove from the first and last pieces, to leave a nice square edge. Cut the two end panels 5in (127mm) square from the ¾in (19mm) pine. Then cut the whitewood moulding to give one 24in (610mm), one 14in (356mm) and two 5¼in (133mm) lengths.

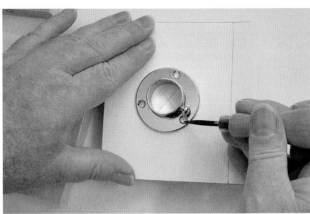

2 Find the position of the rail-end sockets on the two end panels by laying the full-size pattern over the wood. Position the end sockets over the central cross, then use a bradawl to mark pilot holes for the screws; this will make the end sockets easier to fit later.

3 The fourth panel from the left has 6in (152mm) of tongue at the top which is not needed. Saw this off carefully and use it to fill the redundant groove at the top of the second piece from the left, as shown. Sand all the pieces with 180-grit paper on a sanding block, dust off and lay the pieces in order on a flat surface ready for gluing.

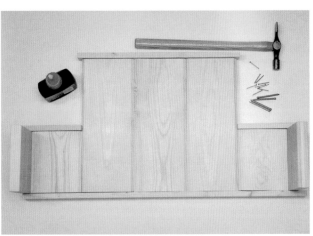

4 Tack the tongue-and-groove pieces together with the small panel pins, then apply glue to the end panels where they meet the back, and tack to secure with the larger pins. Apply glue to the top edging pieces, place each piece in position and tack with ¾in (19mm) panel pins, then turn the whole piece upside down to glue and tack the bottom moulding. Use a nail set to sink the panel pins further into the wood.

5 Leave the work on a flat surface and allow the glue to cure completely. Use a light-coloured wood filler to fill the pinholes, and when dry use a sanding block and 180-grit paper to sand smooth. Remove the dust with a soft brush and a tack cloth. If you want to paint the towel rail, use wood primer, undercoat and topcoat, allowing each coat to dry thoroughly before applying the next; a light rub-down between coats is beneficial.

6 Cut the rail to length so it fits neatly but not too tightly between the end panels. Screw one of the end sockets to an end panel, then, with the rail in position, place the second socket over the other end of the rail and screw into the other end panel. Position the mirror plates on the back, one at each end, and mark pilot holes with a bradawl, then screw into position.

7 Sand the surface of your sheet of birch, using a sanding block with 180-grit paper. Enlarge the motifs from page 123 so the seahorse is 5in (127mm) high, and the fish and starfish 3in (76mm) wide. To save cutting out the two starfish and the two fish separately, tape two pieces of birch together and cut the pair out in one go. Cut out the motifs as described in step 4 on page 124, sand the edges and wipe with a tack cloth.

8 Paint the motifs in pale or bright colours – the choice is yours. We added white to lighten the colours, and acrylic medium to make them slightly transparent. Wipe off the excess, rub down lightly with 320-grit paper when dry, and remove the fine dust with a tack cloth. Apply an acrylic matt varnish and leave to dry. Using good-quality PVA, glue the seahorse and starfish to the front, and the fish to the end panels.

4:3
Tropical fish mobile

This angelfish measures 12 x 9in (305 x 229mm) and is finished in pastel colours. You can make it larger or smaller if you prefer, and use your own choice of colours to complement your own decor. We have cut the pieces up to simplify painting, but if you have a steady hand you could paint the fish as one whole piece – you choose!

You will need:

- Pine, 14 x 8½ x ¾in (355 x 215 x 19mm)
- Small offcut of ¼in (6mm) hardwood dowel
- Scrollsaw and no. 7 blade
- Disc sander
- Drum and flexible-shaft sanders with selection of sanding sleeves
- Sanding block and sandpaper, 180–320 grit
- Pillar drill with ¼in and ¹⁄₆₄in (6 and 0.5mm) bits
- Photocopied patterns
- Carbon paper
- Scissors
- Marking gauge
- Masking tape

- Pencil
- Length of fishing line
- Wood burner
- PVA wood glue
- Glue stick
- Acrylic paints: white and blue
- Acrylic varnish: matt and gloss
- Artists' brushes
- Wax polish
- Soft cloth for buffing
- Tack cloth
- Two-part adhesive such as Araldite
- Cocktail stick

Key point

By enlarging the pattern to different sizes, you could make a whole school of fish. A group of small fish could be hung on wires to make a more elaborate type of mobile in which the individual fish move independently.

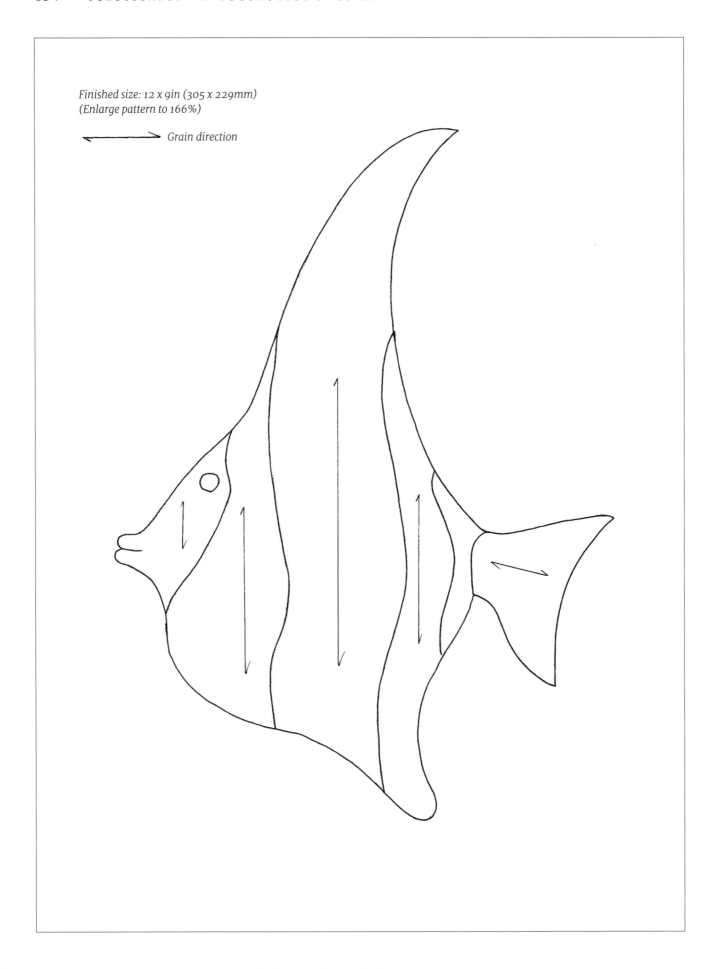

Finished size: 12 x 9in (305 x 229mm)
(Enlarge pattern to 166%)

Grain direction

1 Make three enlarged copies of the pattern – taping two pieces of paper together if necessary – and put one of them aside for later reference. Cut out the body and tail separately and align the two sections of the pattern with the wood grain. A glue stick is best for attaching the pattern to the wood.

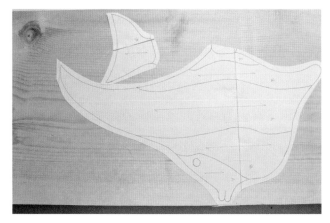

2 Next fit the pillar drill with a ¼ in (6mm) bit, clamp the piece firmly down and drill the hole for the eye.

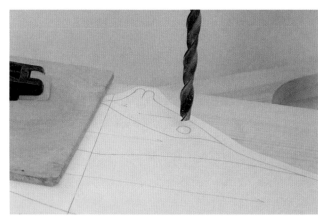

3 There are just two pieces to cut out for the time being. Set up the blade as described on page 17. You will have to cut into the mouth and then back out again to cut from the opposite side; the rest of the outline is straightforward. When both pieces are cut, check that the tail fits accurately onto the body; it is easier to make any adjustment now than when you have started sanding the pieces.

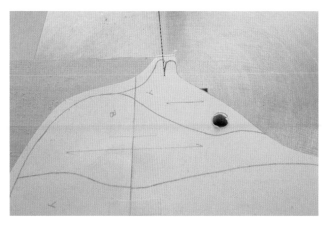

4 Use a marking gauge to scribe a faint centre line all the way around the body and tail of the fish, then highlight this line with a pencil so it's easily visible. This will help you to sand and shape the fish evenly on both sides.

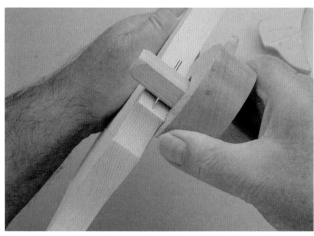

5 Slim down the fins, using the disc sander for fast removal of some of the waste. Then move on to the drum sander to do the more detailed sanding and shaping, using the flexible-shaft sander for the smaller curves. Do not sand away the centre line until you have shaped both sides of the fish evenly. When you are happy with the shape, hand-sand the body and tail pieces to a smooth finish with first 180-grit then 280-grit paper.

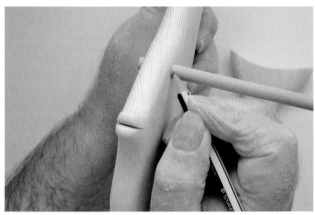

6 Pass a short length of ¼in (6mm) dowel through the eye hole and, using a pencil, mark the shape of the head around both ends of the dowel. Cut the dowel so it projects about ⅛in (3mm) either side of the head, then round over both ends to a smooth finish. Draw a reference line along the length of the rod, so you will know which way round the eye should go when gluing it into place.

7 Use a wood burner to blacken both ends of the dowel. Then cut the dowel in half, to make it easier to hold when applying the gloss varnish.

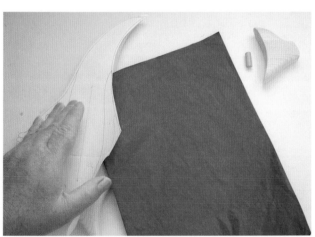

8 Our preference is to cut the fish into separate pieces for painting. Using the extra copy of the pattern with a sheet of carbon paper underneath, trace the inner lines of the fish onto the body. Carefully cut the fish into sections, then remove the burr from the cut lines with 280-grit sandpaper. Wipe all the pieces with a tack cloth to remove the fine dust.

9 Mix the paints with the acrylic medium and apply to the surfaces, then wait a brief moment before wiping off the excess with a lint-free cloth. Allow to dry thoroughly. When dry, lightly rub down with 320-grit sandpaper and again wipe down with a tack cloth, ready for varnishing. Apply an acrylic gloss varnish to the eyes, and matt varnish to everything else. When dry, again give the pieces a very light rubbing down and use the tack cloth to remove the fine dust. Apply wax polish to all pieces except the eye, and then buff to a nice sheen; but be careful not to get any wax on the surfaces to be glued.

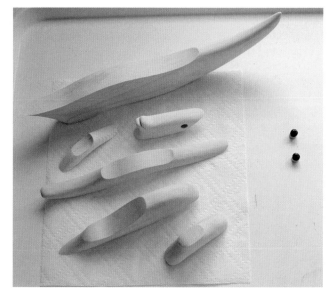

10 First glue the face onto the adjoining blue piece, then lay the largest white piece face downwards on the bench and glue the rear pieces to it, finishing with the tail. Allow these two subassemblies to dry, then apply glue to the two halves, align and press firmly together. Hold in position for a few minutes, then leave supported until the glue has cured. Glue the eyes in place, taking note of your reference mark.

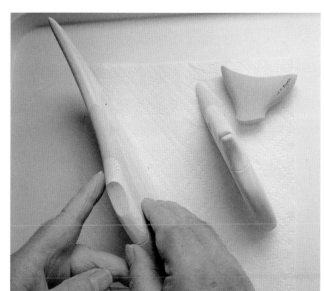

11 Hold the fish between finger and thumb until it hangs correctly, then mark the position with a pencil. Use your smallest drill bit to make the hole for the fishing line; if possible, have another pair of hands available to hold the fish steady. Cut a suitable length of fishing line, and coat one end of it with a two-part glue such as Araldite. Glue the end of a wooden cocktail stick into the hole to wedge it in, and allow to cure completely. Tie a loop in the other end of the line and hang in your chosen spot.

4:4
Bathroom door plate

Create this bathroom door plate so your visitors can easily find the room they want without having to ask. Since there are no words on it, it can be understood by anyone. It takes up the fish motif used in the previous projects, to provide a fully co-ordinated bathroom ensemble.

You will need:
· ¼in (6mm) birch plywood, 12in (305mm) square
· Pine, 12 x 6 x ¾in (305 x 152 x 19mm)
· Scrollsaw with no. 1 and no. 7 blades
· Disc sander
· Drum and flexible-shaft sanders with 120-grit sanding sleeves
· Pencil
· Photocopied patterns
· Pair of compasses
· PVA wood glue
· Glue stick
· Sanding block and sandpaper, 180–320 grit
· Tack cloth
· Artists' brushes
· Acrylic paint: blue, white, parchment and gold
· Acrylic medium
· Acrylic matt varnish
· Clear wax polish
· Hook-and-loop tape with self-adhesive back

Key point

If you happen to have a router and trammel, this provides an easy way to cut out accurate circles; but simply drawing the circle with compasses and cutting it out on the scrollsaw will produce equally good results, if a little care is taken.

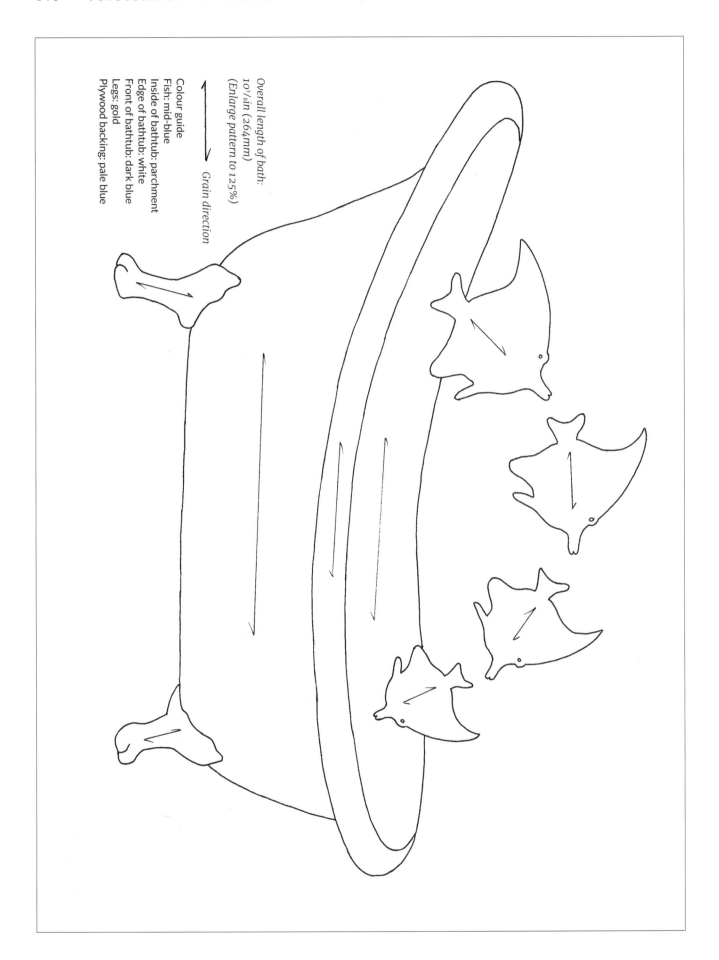

Overall length of bath:
10³/₈in (264mm)
(Enlarge pattern to 125%)

Grain direction

Colour guide
Fish: mid-blue
Inside of bathtub: parchment
Edge of bathtub: white
Front of bathtub: dark blue
Legs: gold
Plywood backing: pale blue

1 First draw a circle of 11½in (292mm) diameter on the plywood and cut it out using a no. 7 blade, aligned and tightened in the usual way. Then make two copies of the bath and fish pattern and cut these into sections, taking note of the grain-direction arrows. Lay the pattern pieces out on the pine so that all the arrows align with the grain of the wood, and attach to the wood using the glue stick.

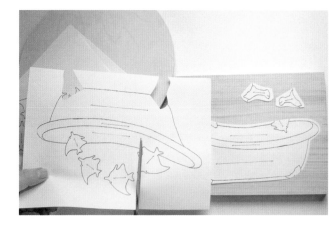

2 Cut out the bathtub, feet and fish from the pine, and check that they all fit together well. Note that the outline of the bath has to be cut into where the fish and the feet overlap it.

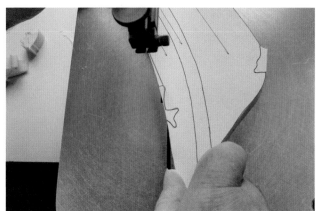

3 Cut the bath into its individual sections and mark in pencil at both ends of the rim where it meets the sides of the bath. Also mark the underside of each piece to ensure that you sand the right side after the pattern has been removed.

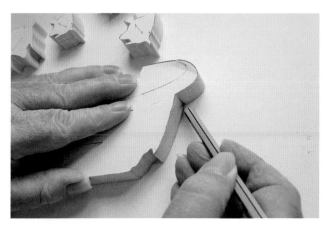

4 Using the disc sander first, lower the side section of the bath by about ¹/₁₆in (2mm), and the inside piece by twice as much. Creating these different height levels will help you when you come to shape the bath with the drum sander.

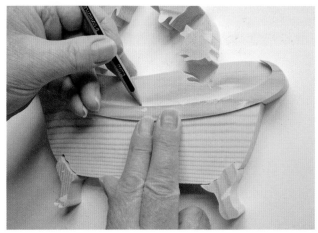

5 Using the drum sander and working with the grain, start to shape the side of the bath. Sand the top surface to remove any scratches left by the disc sander, and then round over the sides and bottom edge, but not the top edge where it joins onto the rim. Sand smooth the piece representing the inside of the bath, and just round over the outer edge a little. Mark the height of these two pieces onto the rim of the bath, then round over the rim on both sides to just above your height marks.

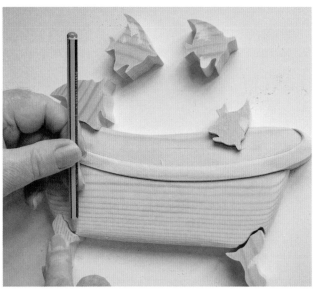

6 Mark the height of the bath pieces onto the adjoining feet and fish; as you sand and shape these pieces, remember not to sand below your height marks.

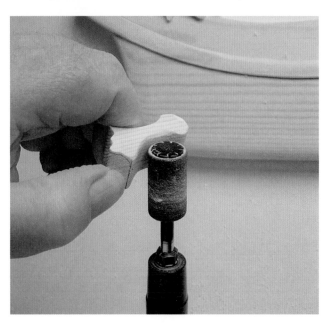

7 A small sanding drum on a flexible-shaft machine is ideal for getting in to the small curves of the fish and feet.

8 Starting with 120-grit paper, and using a sanding block where possible, hand-sand the pieces to smooth any unevenness left by drum sanding. Follow with 180 and then 280-grit paper; a small piece of sandpaper wrapped around a thin dowel will help you with the small curves on the fishes. Also sand the surface of the plywood circle with 180-grit paper on a sanding block. Wipe all parts with a tack cloth to remove the fine dust before colouring.

9 Using a palette to mix the colours with the medium, apply each colour and wait a brief moment before wiping off the excess with a soft cloth to allow the grain to show through. We used only one blue paint, lightening it with a little white for the fish, and with still more white for the circular backing plate.

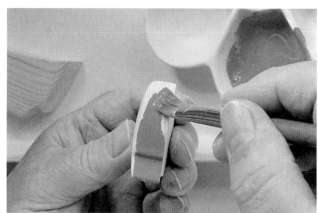

10 Use the same wiping-off process on every piece except the feet of the bath, which are a solid gold colour. Leave to dry thoroughly, then lightly rub down with 320-grit sandpaper. Apply an acrylic matt varnish to all pieces except the gold feet (these will look better shiny) and again leave to dry. A coat of wax polish on the bath and fish will give a nice sheen; don't polish the back plate, or get any on the backs of the other pieces, as this will inhibit gluing.

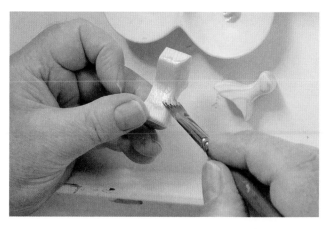

11 Arrange the bath and fish on the back plate until you are satisfied with the layout, then remove each piece in turn and apply good-quality PVA glue. Glue the main bath piece first, then the feet, rim, inside and fish. Press each piece firmly down and allow to dry thoroughly. The door plate is now ready to stick to your bathroom door, using hook-and-loop tape with a self-adhesive back.

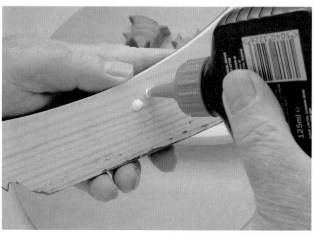

5
Garden Projects

5:4
Wellington boot rack

The projects in Part 5 are suitable for the garden, shed or porch. Assemble them with a water-resistant glue such as weatherproof PVA, and use a good-quality outdoor varnish to protect the surface from the elements. First, here is a space-saving rack for those wet, muddy boots to hang on. We have designed it for children, but we have also given dimensions for a slightly larger version for Mum and Dad's boots; you could decorate this one with motifs chosen from elsewhere in the book if you prefer. The finished rack is simply screwed to the wall, for easy access.

You will need:
- Pine, 18 x 6 x ¾ in (457 x 152 x 19mm), or 24 x 6 x ¾ in (610 x 152 x 19mm) for the adult version
- ¾ in (19mm) hardwood dowel: six pieces 6in (152mm) long, or 7in (178mm) for the adult version
- ⅛in (3mm) mahogany sheet, 5 x 4in (127 x 102mm), for the elephant motifs
- ⅛in (3mm) birch sheet, 6 x 4in (152 x 102mm), for the umbrella motif
- Scrollsaw with no. 7 and no. 1 blades
- Pillar drill and ¾ in (19mm) flatbit
- Pencil
- Ruler
- Photocopied patterns
- PVA wood glue
- Glue stick
- Disc sander (optional)
- Sanding block and sandpaper, 180–320 grit
- Tack cloth
- Artists' brushes
- Acrylic paint: red, white and blue
- Acrylic clear matt varnish
- Wood burner or black waterproof marker pen
- Liquid wax polish
- Soft cloth or brush for buffing
- Bradawl
- Two pairs of mirror plates and fixings
- Phillips screwdriver

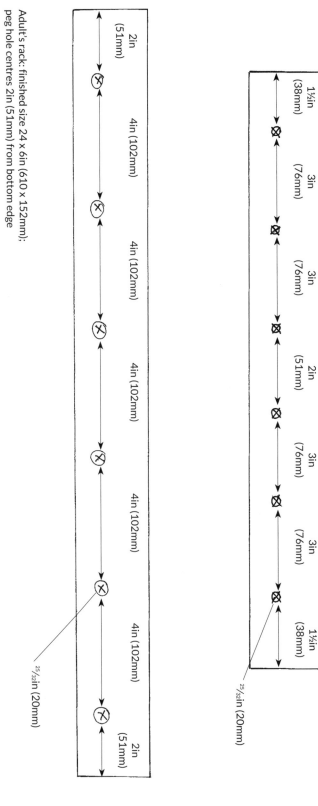

Children's rack: finished size 18 x 6in (457 x 152mm);
peg hole centres 2in (51mm) from bottom edge

1½in (38mm)

3in (76mm)

3in (76mm)

2in (51mm)

3in (76mm)

3in (76mm)

1½in (38mm)

$^{25}/_{32}$in (20mm)

Adult's rack: finished size 24 x 6in (610 x 152mm);
peg hole centres 2in (51mm) from bottom edge

2in (51mm)

4in (102mm)

4in (102mm)

4in (102mm)

4in (102mm)

4in (102mm)

2in (51mm)

$^{25}/_{32}$in (20mm)

Motifs shown actual size

Finished size: 4 ½ x 4 ½in (114 x 114mm)

Finished size: 3¹/₈ x 2in (78 x 51mm)

1 Begin by setting up the scrollsaw with a no. 7 blade, and cutting the backboard to the dimensions given. Use 120, then 180-grit sandpaper on a sanding block to smooth the surfaces and round over the edges.

Next cut the dowels to length: 6in (152mm) for the smaller rack, or 7in (178mm) for the larger. Referring to the pattern, mark out the locations where the holes are to be drilled; their centres are 4in (102mm) from the top edge. A circle template may be helpful.

2 Fit the pillar drill with the ¾in (19mm) flatbit, fasten the backboard firmly to the drill table with two clamps, align the bit with each mark in turn and carefully drill all the way through – make sure you are wearing your safety glasses. Round over one end of each dowel with the disc sander, then hand-sand the ends smooth with 120 and 180-grit sandpaper. Remove the dust with a tack cloth. Lay the backboard on a flat surface and glue in the dowels, removing any glue that may have seeped out with a damp cloth. Allow the glue to cure.

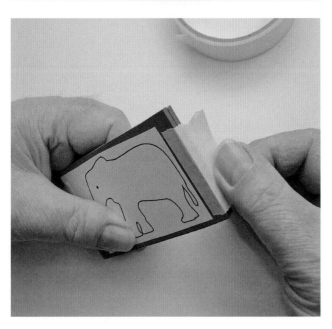

3 Photocopy the motifs, then cut them out and stick them to the wood with the glue stick. Stack-cut the elephants by taping two pieces of the mahogany together. Glue the umbrella pattern to the small piece of birch; we made the handle separately because the wood was not big enough to do it in one piece. Use a no. 1 blade, and if your scrollsaw does not have a zero-clearance insert, make one as described on page 19.

4 With all the motifs cut out, lightly sand the edges with 320-grit sandpaper and then wipe over with a tack cloth. Make the elephants' eyes using a wood burner with a small circular bit, or with a black marker pen.

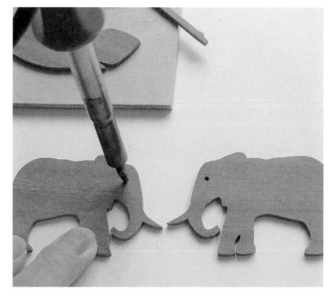

5 The mahogany pieces are best left in their natural state, but the birch umbrella can be painted in whichever colours you wish – not forgetting the edges.

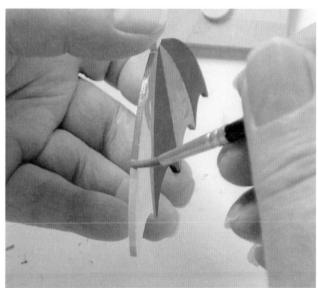

6 Use wood glue to fix the motifs in place, and allow them to dry. Apply an acrylic matt varnish to the boot rack; when dry, lightly rub down with 320-grit sandpaper and again wipe with a tack cloth. Next apply a coat of liquid wax polish and buff to a nice sheen with a cloth or brush. To finish, attach mirror plates at the centre point of each end, and then screw the rack to the wall in a handy location.

Bird house

Make this fun bird house so you can give a home to birds in your garden. Construction is simple, using ¼in (6mm) birch plywood and with a convenient detachable floor panel for easy cleaning. Hang the finished house where it is easily visible from your window, so you and your family can watch the birds come and go.

You will need:
- ¼in (6mm) exterior birch plywood, approx. 24in (610mm) square
- ⅛in (3mm) birch sheet, 8 x 4in (203 x 102mm)
- Small offcut of ¾in (19mm) pine (for ears)
- Six whiskers, cut from a yard broom
- Scrollsaw with no. 5 and no. 1 blades
- Pillar drill and ¹⁄₁₆in (2mm) bit
- Pencil
- Photocopied patterns
- ⅝in (16mm) panel pins
- Pin hammer
- PVA wood glue, weatherproof (water-resistant)
- Glue stick
- Sanding block and sandpaper, 180–320 grit
- Tack cloth
- Artists' brushes and 1in (25mm) household paintbrush
- Exterior wood stain: forest green and antique pine
- Acrylic paint: matt black and white
- Exterior matt varnish
- Bradawl
- 8 screws, ½in no. 4 (12 x 3mm)
- Phillips screwdriver

Key point

Different birds prefer different-sized entrance holes, and a couple of millimetres makes all the difference. Your local wild-bird trust should be able to advise you on this. The size we used is right for blue tits or great tits.

Key point

Any finishes used need to be odourless, non-toxic and environmentally friendly. Read the labels carefully – there are good acrylic products available which fit these requirements.

Bird house:
¼in (6mm) exterior plywood

Parts not shown:
Side panels (make two):
6½ x 4½in (165 x 114mm)
Floor panel: 7 x 6in
(178 x 152mm)
Roof panels: one 6 x 6in
(152 x 152mm),
one 6 x 5¾in
(152 x 146mm)

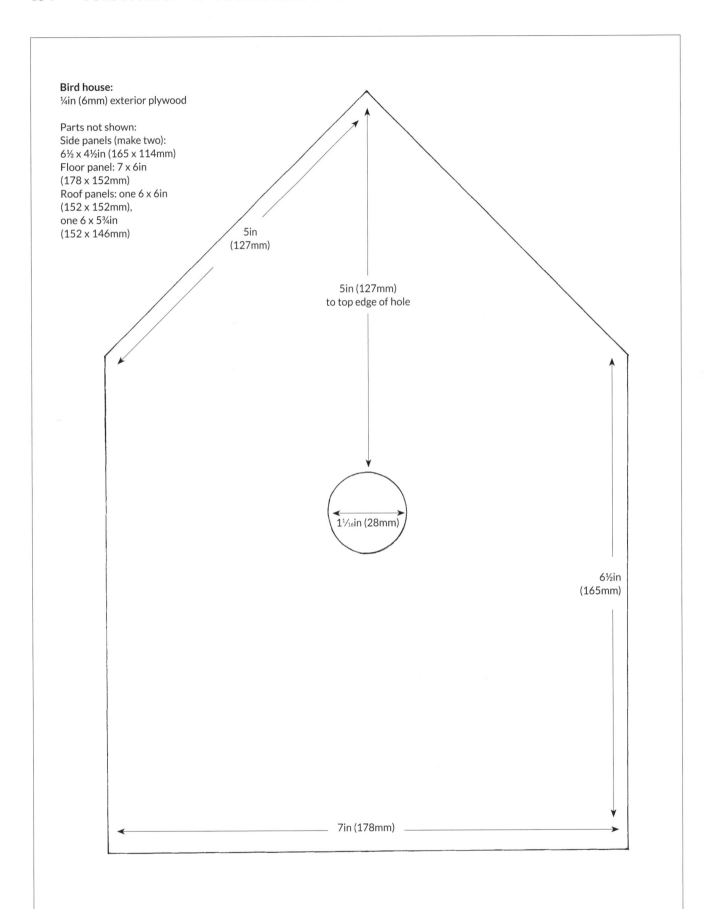

5in
(127mm)

5in (127mm)
to top edge of hole

1¹/₁₆in (28mm)

6½in
(165mm)

7in (178mm)

Bird house ridge pieces
shown actual size

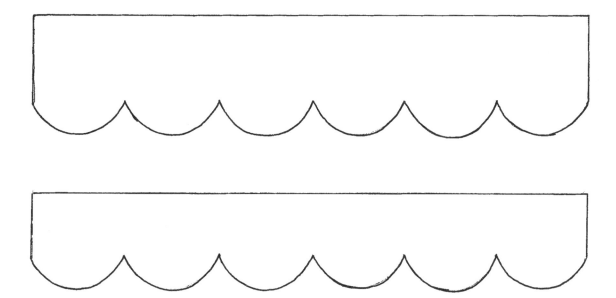

Bird house details
(Enlarge pattern to 141%)

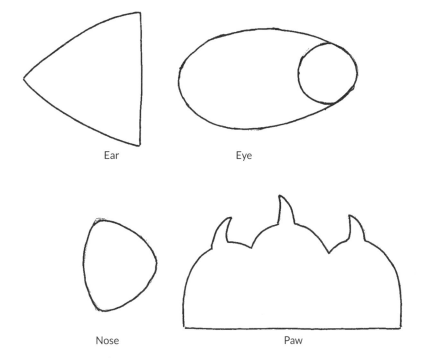

Ear

Eye

Nose

Paw

1 Mark out the nine sections of the bird house – front, back, two sides, floor, two roof panels, two ridge pieces – on the plywood and cut them out with a no. 5 blade. Sand all the edges with a sanding block and 180-grit paper. Drill a ¼in (6mm) hole at the top of the back panel by which to hang the bird house up.

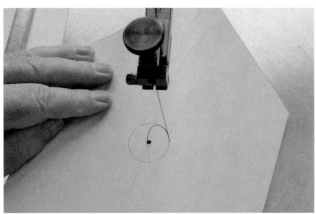

2 The round entrance hole in the front panel can be cut with the scrollsaw if you don't have the right-size drill. Drill a ⅛in (3mm) hole to pass the blade through. Wrap a piece of sandpaper around a length of dowel to sand the entrance smooth – your house guests won't appreciate splinters. Choose outdoor preservative wood stains to paint the bird house, and allow the stain to dry thoroughly before applying a second coat.

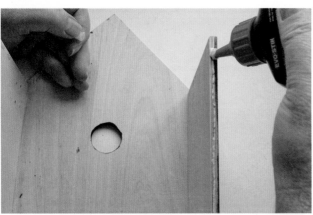

3 Lay the front panel face down on the work surface, and then apply a line of glue down each side close to the edges. Position the two side panels and secure with panel pins, then attach the back panel in the same way and check that everything is square before leaving it to dry.

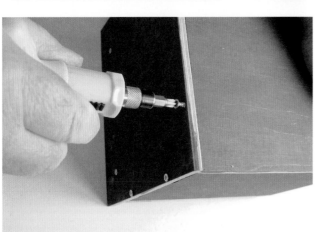

4 Position the house walls on the floor panel so that the floor protrudes beyond the front, then use a pencil to mark the inside edges of the house onto the floor; also mark the outside of the front panel. Drill pilot holes in the floor, two on each side, so it can be screwed on for easy removal when cleaning out – no self-respecting bird will use an old nest left by last year's inhabitants. Attach the floor with eight small screws.

5 Attach the two halves of the roof so that the longer piece just overlaps the shorter one; the back edge is set flush with the back of the house, so the front projects over the entrance. Glue on the decorative ridge pieces, noting in the photograph on page 152 how the joints of roof and ridge are staggered for strength and water-resistance. While the house is drying, make the cat face.

6 Cut the birch into two halves, 4in (102mm) square, and tape them together so the two eyes and two paws can be cut out together (just disregard the extra nose). Use the glue stick to attach the patterns. Glue the ear pattern to the small piece of ¾in (19mm) pine; to save making another copy of the pattern for only the ear, cut this first ear out and then simply trace around it to make one more.

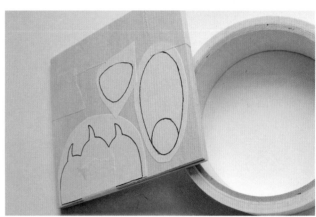

7 With all the pieces cut out, sand around the edges with 280-grit paper to remove the burr, and round over the ears a little if you wish. Wipe over with a tack cloth to remove the dust. Paint the pieces whichever colour you wish – we used black and white to keep it simple. When dry, apply exterior varnish and once more allow to dry.

8 Experiment with the cat's expression: you may like the eyes close together or further apart. When you are satisfied, glue the pieces in place with PVA. The whiskers are just bristles cut from a broom head, with a dab of clear-drying glue to hold them in place. When these pieces are dry, stand the house upright and glue on the ears, using a piece of masking tape to stop them sliding down the roof whilst drying.

Seed organizer

This compartmented seed box is a great gift for the gardener of the house. Easily made, with an uncomplicated construction, it features eye-catching motifs and an interior which is left quite rustic for contrast. The result is an ideal box to store bought and home-gathered seeds alike.

You will need:

- Front and rear panels: pine, two pieces 12 x 3⅛ x 5/16in (305 x 80 x 8mm)
- **Side panels**: pine, two pieces 8 x 3¾ x ¾in (203 x 95 x 19mm)
- Floor: ¼in (6mm) birch plywood, approx. 12 x 7in (305 x 178mm)
- Lid: 5/16in (8mm) tongue-and-groove pine, enough to make up to 12 x 8⅝in (305 x 218mm)
- **Partitions**: pine, two pieces 7¼ x 2 x 3/16in (183 x 51 x 5mm)
- Lid battens: pine, two pieces 6¼ x 1 x 3/16in (158 x 25 x 5mm)
- Floor support: ready-made square-section moulding, 36 x 3/16 x 3/16in (915 x 5 x 5mm)
- ⅛in (3mm) hardwood dowel, two pieces 1in (25mm) long
- Lid prop: whitewood moulding, 8 x ½ x ¼in (203 x 13 x 6mm)
- Motifs: ⅛in (3mm) birch sheet, 16 x 4in (406 x 102mm)
- Scrollsaw with no. 5 and no. 1 blades
- Six Phillips-headed screws, ½in no. 4 (12 x 3mm)
- Phillips screwdriver
- Pillar drill with ⅛in (3mm) and 1/16in (2mm) bits
- Router, or tenon saw and chisel
- Pencil
- Flexible rule or lath
- ⅛in (3mm) hardwood dowel, two pieces 1in (25mm) long
- An adjustable strap, such as used in picture-frame clamps (or adhesive tape, at a pinch)
- Photocopied patterns
- 1in (25mm) and 5/8in (15mm) panel pins
- Pin hammer
- PVA wood glue
- Glue stick
- Sanding block and sandpaper, 180–320 grit
- Tack cloth
- Acrylic artists' brushes
- Acrylic paint: orange, red and green
- Acrylic wood stain: light oak
- Acrylic clear matt varnish
- Liquid wax polish
- Bradawl
- Soft cloth or buffing brush

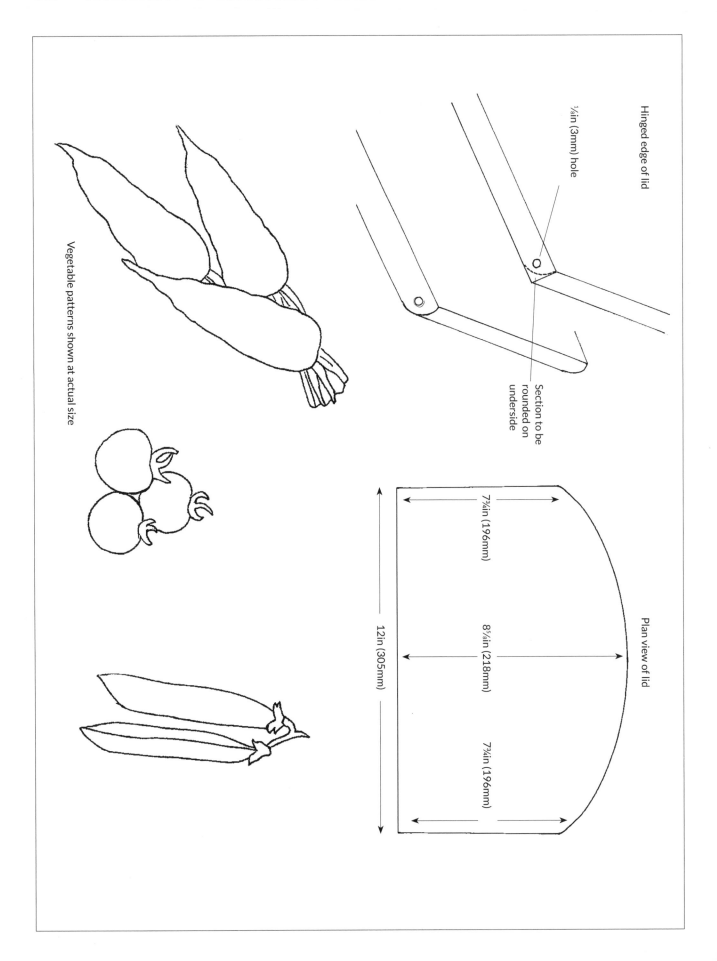

Hinged edge of lid

⅛in (3mm) hole

Section to be rounded on underside

Vegetable patterns shown at actual size

Plan view of lid

7³⁄₄in (196mm)

8⁵⁄₈in (218mm)

7³⁄₄in (196mm)

12in (305mm)

1 Set up the scrollsaw with a no. 5 blade as described on page 17, then, referring to the cutting list on page 159, proceed to cut out the box pieces from your chosen wood.

2 We used tongue-and-groove to make up the lid, and glued and screwed two small battens on the inside to hold it together; if you are using one whole piece of wood you will not need to do this. To make the rounded shape at the front, mark the centre point with a pencil, then bow a flexible ruler back towards the sides and, with the help of another pair of hands, run a pencil line along the shape of the ruler.

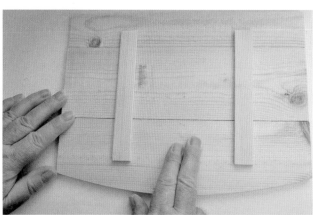

3 The screw holes in the battens are slightly elongated to allow for expansion and contraction.

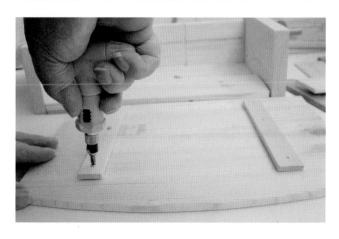

4 When all the pieces are cut out, have a dry assembly of the box to make sure everything fits together. We made the grooves for the partitions with a router, but they could just as easily have been made using a tenon saw and chisel.

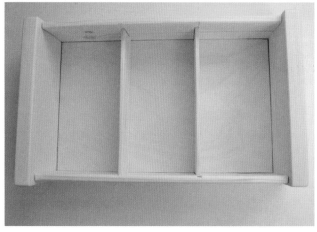

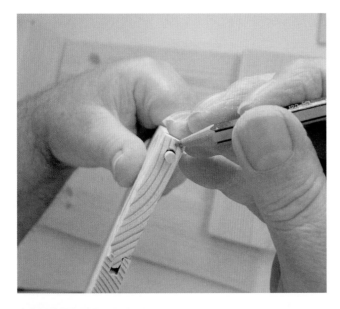

5 The hinge for the lid is simplicity itself. Fit the pillar drill with a ⅛in (3mm) bit, and drill a hole ½in (13mm) deep into either side of the lid and the same distance into both side panels, to take the two 1in (25mm) lengths of dowel.

Mark a quarter-round shape on both ends of the lid, as shown in the drawing, and use this as a guide to sand along the whole length of the back underside edge. Insert the dowels and check that the lid opens freely, without fouling the rear panel.

6 Glue and tack the floor support strips to the bottom inside edge of all four sides. The photo shows two of these fixed; remember that the other two need to be cut a little short so as to fit between these. Apply glue down both inside edges of one side piece and attach the front and rear panels, fitting the plywood floor into position to help keep everything square. Locate the two dowels in the lid and the side panel, then glue the other side panel in the same way, again locating the dowel. Tighten a strap around the box to hold everything together, then use the panel pins and hammer to secure the corners.

7 When the glue has cured, you can slide the partitions into place. Now apply the stain or paint of your choice (we used light oak acrylic wood stain) to the outside of the box, and allow to dry. Lightly rub down with a very fine 320-grit sandpaper, then wipe over with a tack cloth to remove the fine dust. Apply a coat of acrylic matt varnish and once again leave to dry. We made a simple prop for the lid out of whitewood moulding, 8 x ½ x ¼in (203 x 13 x 6mm).

8 Photocopy the vegetable patterns and cut them out. Roughly mark the length of the carrots onto the birch sheet, then cut the birch to length with a no. 1 blade. Cut the remaining birch in half, then, using the glue stick, glue the carrot pattern onto the first piece. Position the peas and tomatoes on the second piece and then tape the third piece to the underside, so you can stack-cut both sets of peas and tomatoes together.

9 If you do not have a zero-clearance insert, make one as described on page 19. Proceed to cut out the motifs; for the small gap between the tomatoes you will need to drill a ¹⁄₁₆in (2mm) hole and thread the blade through. When the motifs are cut out, remove the tape and the patterns, and lightly sand the edges with 320-grit paper to take off the burr. Wipe the pieces over with a tack cloth to remove the fine dust.

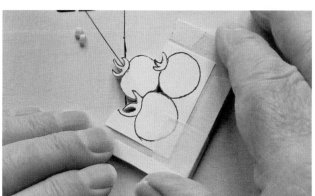

10 Referring to the patterns, transfer or copy the dividing lines between the individual vegetables. Paint the carrots orange, the tomatoes red and the main part of the peas a medium green, then darken the green paint by adding an even darker green or a tad of black, to paint the stalks and carrot tops dark green. When the paint is dry, draw over the dividing lines with a fine brown or black felt-tip pen.

11 Varnish the vegetables and again allow to dry, then glue them on with good-quality PVA. When dry, apply a coat of liquid wax polish to the whole box and buff with a buffing brush to a nice sheen. We repeated one of the poppies from page 55 to make a surprise motif on the underside of the lid.

5:4
Squirrel name plate

This unique and eye-catching squirrel supporting a house name or number plate would look impressive hanging at the front of any house. Rather than fill the pages with examples of various letter styles, we have left the choice of font to you: there are countless ones to choose from in craft pattern books and on the Internet, or you can use one of the fonts available on your computer. Of course, there is nothing to stop you simply drawing your own letters.

You will need:
- Pine, 24 x 7½ x ¾in (610 x 191 x 19mm)
- ¼in (6mm) birch plywood, 14in (356mm) square
- For the name plate: pine, 12 x 3¾ x ¾in (305 x 95 x 19mm)
- For the letters: ⅛in (3mm) mahogany or birch sheet, 6 x 4in (152 x 102mm)
- Scrollsaw with no. 7 and no. 1 blades
- Disc sander
- Drum sander
- PVA wood glue
- Photocopied patterns
- Glue stick
- Sanding block and sandpaper, 120–320 grit
- Masking tape
- Artists' brushes
- Acrylic wood stains: cherry, cedar, Old English oak and white
- Acrylic matt black paint
- Black marker pen
- Pencil
- Ruler
- Exterior varnish
- Short length of chain and four eyelets
- D-ring and screw or screws
- Bradawl
- Phillips screwdriver

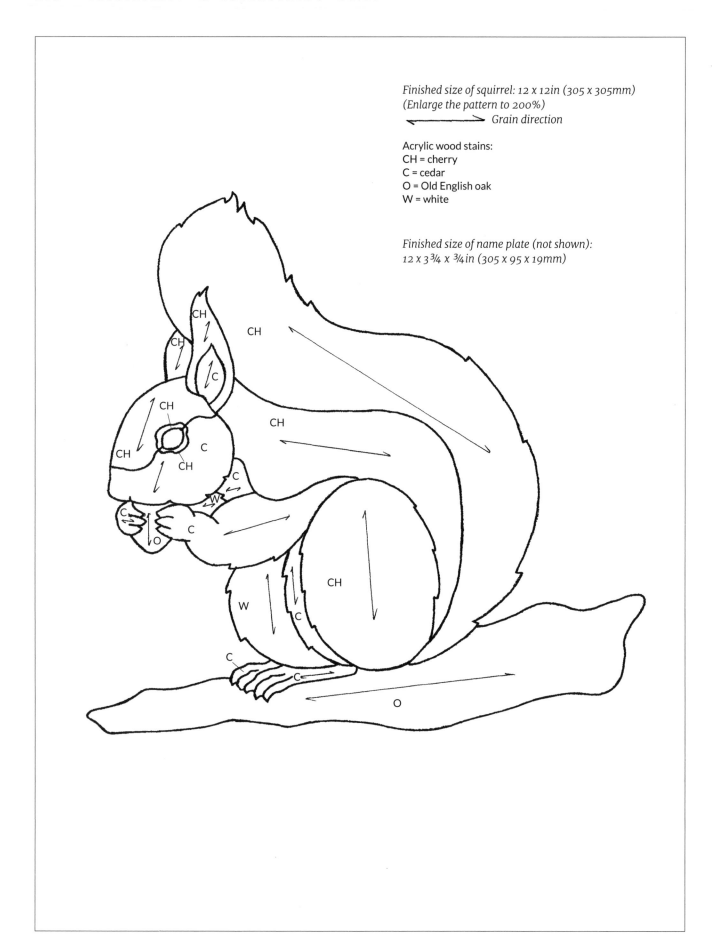

Finished size of squirrel: 12 x 12in (305 x 305mm)
(Enlarge the pattern to 200%)
Grain direction

Acrylic wood stains:
CH = cherry
C = cedar
O = Old English oak
W = white

Finished size of name plate (not shown):
12 x 3¾ x ¾in (305 x 95 x 19mm)

1 Enlarge the squirrel pattern to 12 x 12in (305 x 305mm), taping two sheets of paper together if necessary, and make six photocopies. Cut the patterns into six sections according to the grain direction arrows, and align each section with the grain of your wood. When you are happy with the layout, attach the patterns to the wood using the glue stick.

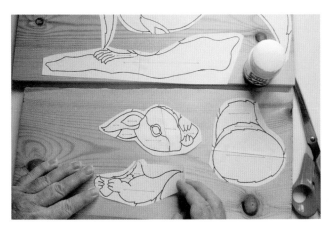

2 Fit the scrollsaw with a no. 7 blade, aligned and adjusted as described on page 17. Before cutting, make sure your wood is flat. Start by cutting out the hind leg and tummy piece, then the arm section, checking the fit of each component against the adjoining pieces as you go. Mark the underside of each piece, to ensure that you sand the right side later on.

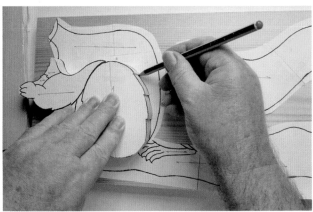

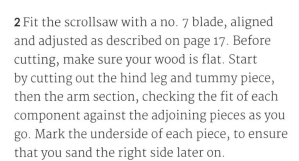

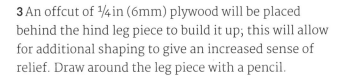

3 An offcut of ¼in (6mm) plywood will be placed behind the hind leg piece to build it up; this will allow for additional shaping to give an increased sense of relief. Draw around the leg piece with a pencil.

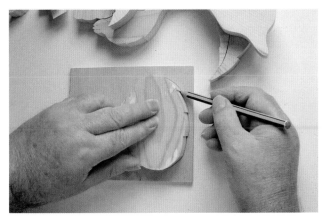

4 Cut just inside the pencil line so the backing piece will fit easily into place.

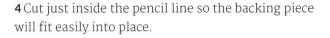

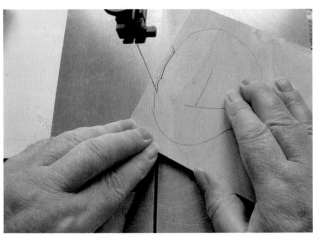

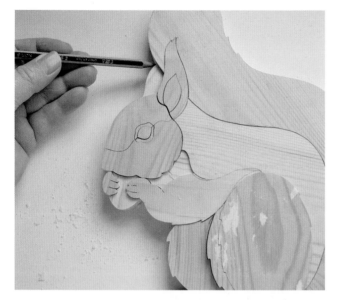

5 Use the disc sander to sand down the branch, nut and right ear pieces by ⁵/₃₂in (4mm), and the inside chest pieces by ¹/₈in (3mm). Reducing these key pieces will help give the squirrel a three-dimensional appearance and make it easier to sand and shape the adjoining pieces.

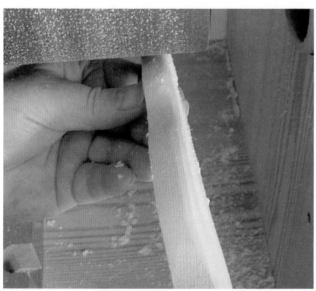

6 Use the drum sander to round over the outside edges of the branch, working with the grain and following the contours of the wood. Then, using a sharp pencil, mark the height of the branch onto all the adjoining pieces: foot, hind leg and tail.

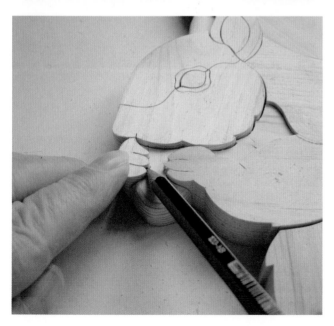

7 Sand and shape round the nut and right ear pieces, and again mark the height onto all adjoining parts. Shape the tail by rounding over the outside edges, lowering it more toward the top, so the left ear stands higher by approximately ¹/₃₂–¹/₁₆in (1–2mm). Be careful not to sand below your height marks for the right ear and branch pieces. Sand the outer edge of the tummy round, and then transfer the sanded shape onto the foreleg. The foreleg and back pieces need hardly any sanding at all.

8 Sand down the inner ear by approximately ¹/₃₂in (1mm), so it's lower than the outer ear piece. Mark the height of all the pieces around the head and then hold the two pieces of the head together while you sand the edges round. As you sand the remaining pieces try to visualize the shape of the squirrel; if you're unsure how much to take off, sand a little at a time and try the piece in position before sanding further.

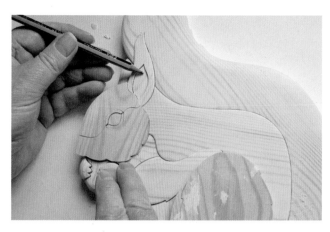

9 When you are happy with the shape, hand-sand the pieces, first with 120-grit paper to remove the imperfections from the drum sanding, then moving on to 180 and 280-grit for a really smooth finish. Remove the dust with a soft brush, followed by a tack cloth.

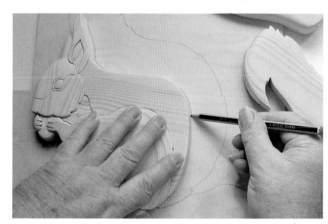

10 Assemble all the pieces together onto the ¼in (6mm) plywood, then using a sharp pencil trace all around the outside edge. Now remove the six main sections one at a time so that you can trace around the remaining pieces

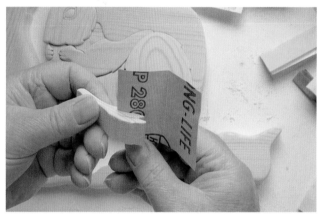

11 Change the scrollsaw blade for a no. 5 and proceed to cut out the backing. Apply a sanding sealer to the back, and an acrylic matt black paint all around the edge to give a more finished look.

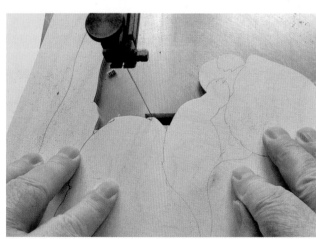

12 Use a thick black marker pen to go over your pencil lines, so that if you do have any small gaps between the pieces they will not be so noticeable to the eye.

13 Following the colour guidelines on the pattern, apply the wood stains to the appropriate pieces. After colouring each piece, wait a brief moment and then remove the excess stain with a soft cloth. This will eliminate any brush marks, so all you see is the grain of the wood. Allow the pieces to dry completely, then very lightly sand with 320-grit paper and use the tack cloth to remove the dust. Apply a coat of exterior varnish to all the pieces and again allow to dry. The unstained piece is the plywood backing for the hind leg.

14 Lay out the pieces in order for gluing. Start at the bottom by gluing on the branch, then move upward until all the pieces are securely stuck down. Don't forget the plywood packing piece behind the hind leg. Wipe away any glue that may have seeped out with an old acrylic brush and a damp cloth. Leave the squirrel on a flat surface until the glue has cured.

15 We made our pine name plate 12 x 3¾ x ¾ in (305 x 95 x 19mm). Sand with 120-grit paper on a sanding block, slightly rounding the edges, then change to 180-grit for a smoother finish. Once you have chosen from the countless fonts available – or designed your own – write out the name you require and use the photocopier to enlarge or reduce it to fit the size of the name plate. Choose between dark letters on a light background or light on dark.

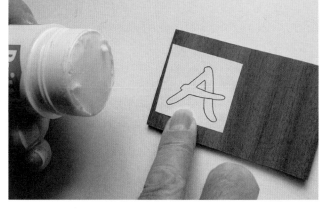

16 Fit the scrollsaw with a no. 1 blade, and attach a false plywood table if you do not have a zero-clearance insert. Cut out the letters, remove the paper patterns and lightly sand the top and edges with 320-grit sandpaper.

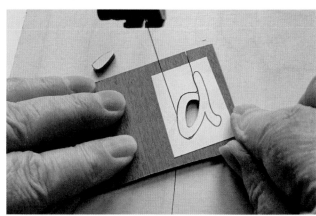

17 Carefully arrange the letters or numbers on the name plate, then remove one at a time and glue into place. Allow the glue to cure, then apply a coat of exterior varnish and again leave to dry.

18 Screw a stout D-ring to the back of the squirrel. Attach four hooks or eyelets – two on the underside of the branch and two on the top of the name plate – then run two short lengths of chain between the eyelets so the name plate hangs freely. Now all that remains is to hang it outside your house.

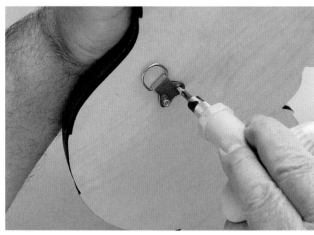

Internet resources

This list is intended to get you started in your search for further information, and does not claim to be exhaustive. Though every effort has been made to ensure that information is correct at the time of going to press, please note that company names and web addresses do change from time to time.

Organizations and clubs

Scroll Saw Goodies
www.scrollsawgoodies.com
Projects, pattern making, forums

Scrollsaw Association of the World
www.saw-online.com
A comprehensive site where you can find out everything to do with the scrollsaw, from woods to patterns

Scroll Saw Village
www.scrollsawvillage.com
A community of scrollsaw enthusiasts with forums, pattern library, gallery etc.

Scrollsaw manufacturers

Axminster Power Tool Centre
www.axminster.co.uk

Craftsman
www.sears.com

Dremel
www.dremeleurope.com

Delta
www.deltamachinery.com
www.toolbank.com

DeWalt
www.dewalt.com

Genesis
www.gensispowertools.com

Hawk
www.rbiwoodtools.com

Hegner UK
www.hegner.co.uk

Jet
http://www.jettools.com/us/en/

Proxxon
www.proxxon.com

PS Wood Machines
www.pswood.com

Shop Fox
www.woodstockint.com

Seyco, Excalibur
www.seyco.com

Scheppach
www.scheppach.com

SIP
www.sip-group.com

WEN
http://www.wenproducts.com

Tool and material suppliers

Always Hobbies
www.alwayshobbies.com
Craft kits, materials, tools, etc.

Axminster Power Tool Centre
www.axminster.co.uk
An Aladdin's cave of hand and power tools

Cherry Tree – Wildwood
www.cherrytreetoys.com
Scrollsaw patterns, blades, tools and so much more!

Jim Dandy
www.jimdandy.com

Liquitex
www.liquitex.com
Sometimes you need colour and here you will find it all

Olson Saw Co.
www.olsonsaw.net
The Olson reverse skip-tooth blade is our personal choice

Rapid Resizer
www.rapidresizer.com
Resize existing patterns/designs or make you own

S. L. Hardwoods
www.slhardwoods.co.uk
Hardwoods from a managed source, tools etc.

Glossary

Disc sander
A sanding machine in which abrasive paper is fixed to a rotating disc; useful for thicknessing and flattening wood.

Drum sander
A cylindrical sanding device fitted to an electric drill or flexible-shaft tool; useful for shaping curved surfaces and edges.

Fretsaw
(1) an older name for the scrollsaw; (2) a hand-held saw with a narrow blade fitted to a metal frame, used for cutting intricate curves by hand.

Hold-down arm
An accessory resembling the foot of a sewing machine, which helps to stabilize the work and acts to some extent as a safety guard.

Pin-end blade
A blade secured to the scrollsaw by means of pins passing through both ends; usually available only in larger sizes.

Plain-end blade
A blade which is secured to the scrollsaw by means of clamps; available in many varieties.

Reverse-tooth blade
A blade in which the lower teeth face upwards, to minimize tear-out on the underside of the work.

Skip-tooth blade
A blade with spaces between the teeth to improve the sawdust clearance and allow faster cutting.

Spiral blade
A blade whose teeth are wound spirally around a central axis, to permit cutting in any direction.

Stack-sawing
Cutting more than one layer of material at a time, so as to produce a pair or set of matching pieces.

Standard blade
A blade in which all teeth point downwards.

Table
The flat cast-iron or aluminium platform that supports the work on the scrollsaw during cutting.

Throat
The space between the blade and the arm support at the back of the scrollsaw.

TPI
Teeth per inch (25mm): the traditional measurement of the coarseness or fineness of a saw blade.

Zero-clearance insert
A removable plug that fills the blade hole in the scrollsaw table, to provide additional support to the workpiece and prevent small parts from falling through.

Index

About the authors

Julie and Fred Byrne have been actively interested in woodworking for over 20 years, but it was not until they saw a demonstration at a woodworking show that they realized just how versatile a tool the scrollsaw could be. It was not long before they bought their first scrollsaw and a selection of good books on the subject, and started to discover its possibilities for themselves. They have now been hooked on this fascinating craft for many years, and their distinctive and original designs have featured regularly in woodworking magazines.

Acknowledgements

We would like to thank Mark Cass for encouraging us to write this book, Stephen Haynes for his greatly appreciated input, and especially Benità and Sam for their much-valued help and support in writing the book. Without them it would have been much harder. Thank you!

Guild of Master Craftsman Publications Ltd,
Castle Place, 166 High Street, Lewes, East Sussex, BN7 1XU, United Kingdom
Tel: +44 (0)1273 488005
www.gmcbooks.com

Ask us for a complete catalogue, or visit our website.